D1149473

THE PROMISED LAND

A Guide to Positive thinking for Sufferers of Stress, Anxiety, and Depression

Dr. Rick Norris

authorHOUSE™

1663 LIBERTY DRIVE, SUITE 200
BLOOMINGTON, INDIANA 47403
(800) 839-8640
WWW.AUTHORHOUSE.COM

First published by AuthorHouse 6/9/2006

ISBN: 1-4208-9582-6 (sc)

Printed in the United States of America
Bloomington, Indiana

This book is printed on acid-free paper.

This book is dedicated to all the people I have had the privilege of helping over the years. You have all been brave enough to face your demons and come through stronger than you were before, I salute you.

Dr Rick Norris

Further copies of this book can be obtained online from authorhouse.co.uk or from Amazon. co.uk or by order from Waterstones.

ABOUT THE AUTHOR.

Rick is a Chartered Psychologist who works in both clinical and occupational settings. He is a Consultant Psychologist at the Manor Hospital in Walsall where he counsels clients with stress, anxiety and depression.

Rick is a visiting lecturer at Warwick University where he lectures to students in the Centre for Primary Health Care Studies. He also works as a consultant for a range of organisations in occupational environments and his clients include Compaq, Nokia, Unisys, Hewlett-Packard, the Terrance Higgins Trust and a number of SMEs.

His book 'The Promised Land' is a distillation of the simple theories and concepts he has used to help hundreds of individuals suffering from psychological distress over the last 10 years. Professionally his main interest is helping people to lead more fulfilled lives.

Born in 1959 in Portsmouth, Rick is divorced with three children, Sam, Jack and Martha, apart from his family his main interests are running and keeping fit; reggae music, horse-racing and warm climates. He is also a long-suffering Pompey fan.

Rick can be contacted on ricnorris1@aol.com.

ACKNOWLEDGEMENTS.

Writing is generally a fairly solitary pastime but almost every author receives a lot of help and support from friends and family, and I'm no different. So to the following people a big **thank you**:

To my Dad who took the time to cast his experienced eye over the boy's work, your kind comments were much appreciated.

To my sister Alexandra who let me stay in her home in the south of France where some of the book was written, it's no wonder I didn't want to go home, the food, wine and ambience were very conducive to writing.

To my brother Damien the priest, who said some prayers for the success of the book (well, it would have been silly not to use the family connection).

To my children Sam, Jack and Martha who were kind enough to be impressed with their old man's efforts.

To my friend Sue Wolton, who generously gave her time to read and re-read the manuscript, your suggestions were extremely helpful and they improved my writing no end.

To my sister Josi, who helped me see how difficult life can be for some people, a valuable lesson for writing this guide.

To Kate Fennel, from the Manor Hospital in Walsall, who unwittingly gave me the idea for writing the book in the first place.

To Tris Ross who helped me with the technical side and sent numerous images back and forth.

Thanks, Rick.

TABLE OF CONTENTS

INTRODUCTION.

If you, or someone you care about, is experiencing some form of psychological distress then hopefully this book will be able to help.

'The Promised Land' is about providing a framework for understanding the causes of psychological distress as well as a practical means of overcoming it. By assisting individuals to overcome psychological distress we can help them to become more fulfilled in every aspect of their lives. The aim of this book is to try to lead people on a journey to their own Promised Land.

Before we start the journey, I'd like to explain a little more about this book. At the beginning of my favourite film, "Butch Cassidy and the Sundance Kid", the following statement is made: "Most of what follows is true……"

It's the same with this book. It explains how I've tried to help people who have been suffering from anxiety, stress and depression. I've spent many years as a psychologist counselling people suffering from various forms of emotional distress and some of their stories are recorded in the book. Although the details have been changed to protect their identities, all the stories are based on real life experiences. This isn't an academic textbook, although there are some references to follow up if you want more information on certain subjects. This is a book which is aimed at giving people a simple understanding of how we all experience negative emotions which have the potential to be seriously debilitating to both our physical and psychological well-being. The book is my best attempt at explaining, in simple everyday terms, what sometimes happens in our minds that can lead us to suffer from psychological distress. However, it's only my explanation. Feel free to challenge my thoughts and beliefs and maybe you'll develop a better theory that helps you to understand these problems.

Whenever I've worked with people during counselling I've tried to explain things in straightforward terms: I use stories and analogies that people can relate to and I've reproduced these in this book. I also find that using diagrams can help clients see things visually, so I've jotted down the diagrams in this book too. In all my sessions I give people homework. I always tell clients that we can only achieve so much in one hour, but if they do their homework between sessions we can achieve so much more. I've reproduced some of the homework exercises, and there are blank sheets at the end of the book to write down your own thoughts. Be bold; don't be afraid of writing all over the pages of this book. Underline the bits that strike a chord; make notes on the subjects that you want to reflect on later; capture your own thoughts as you go along.

The main thrust of the book is about the relationship between self-doubt and negative self-fulfilling prophecies whereby people fail in various aspects of their life simply because they believe that they *will* fail. In my experience of counselling, self-doubt is the biggest problem that most of the people I've worked with suffer from. In this book we will look at the links between self-doubt, lack of confidence, low levels of self-esteem, pessimism, negative thought patterns and self-fulfilling prophecies. If we can overcome our self-doubt and develop our confidence and self-esteem then we will be able to live more fulfilled lives.

Most of the help in this book is actually pretty simple. However, that doesn't mean it's easy to put into practice. My job is to help people re-train their minds to think more positively, but improvements only come with practice. To succeed we have to work hard. To change our thinking patterns requires a big effort, but if we keep making the effort the outcome will be worth it.

Many of the people I've worked with have said that experiencing anxiety, stress or depression is far worse than having a physical ailment like a broken arm. Everyone can see a broken arm and most people are very sympathetic. No one says, "Pull yourself together". Once the broken arm has been re-set, and the initial pain has subsided, we can get on with life reasonably well until it heals. Because a broken arm is very tangible, it would never occur to anyone that we might be 'swinging the lead' whilst we're off sick. It doesn't take a lot of mental, or physical, effort to heal a broken arm: the body heals itself, and with some physiotherapy, we're soon back to normal.

Unfortunately, most forms of psychological ailment are more complex than physical problems and many people unsympathetically believe that we bring these problems on ourselves. In a sense we do, but it isn't a conscious choice to become stressed, anxious or depressed. William Glasser (1) uses depression as a verb. He suggests that we subconsciously choose to depress. This may be a slight over simplification, but, as we will see later, emotional distress occurs because of our thought patterns, and ultimately we are responsible for our own thoughts. We can either let our mind control us, or we can choose to control our mind.

The idea that we sub-consciously choose our psychological and emotional distress is a challenging thought for many sufferers. However, by accepting the view that we can control our thought patterns we give ourselves the power to combat the negative thoughts that can be so destructive.

This book isn't intended to replace face to face counselling. However, not everyone feels able to work with a counsellor, and even if they do, it can be expensive and difficult to get an appointment. At the risk of sounding over confident, I know that the theories and exercises in this book have worked for most of my clients. They work for three reasons. Firstly, because the explanations give my clients the clarity they need to understand what is going on in their minds. Secondly, because the practical exercises and techniques are not difficult to complete. Lastly, and most importantly, because my clients keep practising the techniques.

CHAPTER 1.
LIFE - NOT FOR THE FAINT HEARTED.

At the start of one episode of the TV series 'Cheers' the character Norm walks into the bar. Woody the barman calls out "Hi Norm, how's life?" To which Norm replies "Not for the fainthearted." Norm is right, life can be very daunting at times and one of the reasons it's become so daunting for many people is that in the 21st century we now live in a very complex world. Our expectations of life have increased. The expectation is driven from our own views, the views of our family, friends and work colleagues; and also by the messages put out by an ever increasingly powerful media which influences so many aspects of our lives. The complexity of our 21st century world and the increase in our expectations is partly to blame for the huge rise in the amount of psychological distress people experience. So, before we talk more specifically about anxiety, stress and depression this chapter will focus briefly on why it's such a common modern day phenomenon.

The world of work.
Our relationship with our work is a useful example of how things have changed in recent times. Most people work. The work isn't always paid work - bringing up children, voluntary work, going to school or college, and helping in community activities are all work. Work is a central part of our lives. Life affects work and work affects life. The world of work is symptomatic of society in general and the world of work has changed radically in the last fifty years.

Whenever I'm training groups of Occupational Health professionals our discussions often centre on the question of what makes a good place to work. The answer to this question seems to be that our work place should help to feed our motivation: not just for the actual work itself, but more broadly, it should feed our motivation for life.

In the 1950s people lived to work and it was fairly typical for people to maintain their jobs over a lifetime. There were fewer choices and people worked to ensure that they had sufficient money to meet their basic needs. Fifty years ago it wasn't uncommon for someone to spend their entire career with one employer. In the 21st century it's very different. John Schwartz (1) in a recent article on workplace stress in the New York Times quoted the research of Richard Sennett, a sociologist at New York University, who calculated that the average American with two years of college education will change jobs eleven times before retirement.

In the 1950s work was seen as a means to an end. The end was survival; people lived to work. Today the pendulum has swung to the other extreme. Many people now work to live and have chosen lifestyles that reflect this. People want to take advantage of all the opportunities that exist in life. Family, leisure, travel and our physical and spiritual well being are increasingly viewed as more important than work for many people. Our expectations of life have been raised and therefore it's not surprising that our expectations of work have also been increased.

Motivation.
Much of the research on motivation seems to support the hypothesis that our expectations of life generally, and work in particular, have increased. One of the earliest theories of motivation is the often-quoted work of Abraham Maslow (2). Maslow suggested that there is a hierarchy of needs that have to be satisfied in the following order:

1. The most basic needs are the physical needs to sustain life.
2. The next step up the hierarchy is the need for safety and security.
3. Following these is the need for belonging and love.
4. Then we have the need for self-esteem.
5. Finally the need for self-actualisation – to become the best person we can be.

Maslow's work has stood the test of time well, although some people argue that these needs do not have to be satisfied sequentially. We can point to the example of people who are able to maintain their self-esteem and even becoming self-actualised despite being in extreme situations where their lower order needs such as safety and security are not being met. For example the round the world yachtswoman Ellen MacArthur would be an example of this, alone with only the most basic food rations and in constant danger from the elements her self-esteem and self-actualisation were still being fed by her chosen 'work'.

The industrialisation of the western world lies at the heart of what came to be known as 'modern' society. This was exemplified by the car factories which sprang up in Detroit in the USA and the term "Fordism" was used to describe the relationship between work and life where employers assumed the main source of motivation for their workforce was financial incentive rather than intrinsic job satisfaction (3). The phrase 'wage slave' refers to the notion that work is simply an activity that gives us the financial means to sustain our lives.

However, in the 21st century we have come to expect more from life than just a basic existence. Simple monetary reward is not enough to feed our motivation. We need to have our higher level needs met, we need to feed our minds not just our stomachs.

This is reflected in more recent theories of motivation. William Glasser (4) suggests that we have four genetic needs that have to be satisfied:
Love and Belonging
Control (Power)
Freedom
Fun/Excellence

None of Glasser's genetic needs relate to the most basic needs on Maslow's hierarchy. They all point to the higher level needs. This theme is also present in Tam's (5) work on shared values, which suggest that the elements in life we value the most are:

Love
Wisdom
Justice
Fulfillment

Once again, this seems to point to higher order needs being the most significant ones. The work of Glasser and Tam probably reflect the fact that, in the west, most of our basic needs are met at a far higher level than they were in the early days of industrialisation. Today few people die of starvation or exposure to the elements because they don't have a roof over their heads. In the West we live in a relatively affluent society. Because of this we have moved from a modern society to a 'post-modern' society where we now want our higher level needs met in both our personal lives and in the workplace.

It goes without saying that we still want to feel safe and secure and have sufficient money to provide a decent standard of living, but in our post-modern world we want more than this. We want fulfilling, reciprocal relationships with people who show us appreciation, respect and care. We want to be consulted and involved in the decisions that affect our lives. We want the opportunity to use and develop our talents. We want to feel that we add value and make a difference.

Sickness absence and stress.
Despite the facts that modern workplaces are safer than ever and we are, in relative terms, far better off than our parents or grandparents, we continue to see worrying trends in sickness absence from work. An increasing number of days are lost through various forms of psychological distress each year. Stress was cited as the second biggest cause of sickness absence for non-manual workers in the

UK for the year 2002-2003 (6). Many of these cases end up in long term sickness, which accounts for around 13 million days' absence and costs the UK £3.8 billion (7).

The reasons for this increase seem to be twofold; firstly, some workplaces are not good places to work because they do not feed people's higher level motivational needs. Good places to work have fun, flexible, balanced environments where the work practices reflect this. The emphasis is on employee participation in decision making, self-development and providing a fairer more equitable way of rewarding people for their efforts. However, even in very positive work environments some employees still take time off work through psychological distress and this is due to the second reason for the spiralling long term sickness – people's higher level needs are not being met outside work.

Life affects work and work affects life.
Our increased expectations of life put greater pressure on us and with the added pressure sometimes the cracks begin to show. Perhaps we are our own worst enemies; maybe our expectations are simply unrealistically high. For example, relationships seem to break down with far greater frequency than they used to, separation and divorces are more commonplace now than they've ever been. In the UK in 1961 there were just over 27,000 divorces, in 2003 there were over 166,000 (8). Life affects work and work affects life. Dissatisfaction at home spills into our work life and vice-versa.

Organisations can help their employees by adopting work practices that help feed their people's motivation, but changing a company's philosophy is difficult and this book isn't about organisational change and development. Reflecting on our relationship with work simply demonstrates how society has changed in the last fifty years. The changes in society have made life more difficult for many people, as Norm said; life is not for the fainthearted. Hopefully this chapter provides a framework for understanding why we seem to be far more prone to psychological distress than fifty years ago. The subsequent chapters will describe the effects of psychological distress in a very practical way and ultimately, what we can do to try to manage our distress effectively.

Summary of Chapter 1. Life – not for the fainthearted.

The world of work.
Society has changed quite radically over the last 50 years and the world of work reflects these societal changes. We have an increasingly complex relationship with our employer and far higher expectations of work than our grandparents had. This has contributed to people experiencing greater levels of dissatisfaction, which in turn, has lead to higher levels of psychological distress.

Motivation.
Most models of motivation suggest that some of the most important motivational needs are our higher level needs i.e. self-esteem and self-actualisation. Recent models make very little reference to lower level needs such as our physical needs. This is probably due to the fact that in western society most of these needs are already met, if not by our employer, then by the welfare state. Consequently, in the 21st century we want society, and the world of work, to feed our motivation, not just our stomachs.

Sickness absence and stress.
The statistics seem to suggest that sickness due to psychological distress is on the increase. The increase in psychological ill-health would appear to be due in no small part to the levels of dissatisfaction that people experience with their lives. Whilst people have always had to contend with psychologically challenging situations such as death, job loss and the break up of relationships, the incidence of psychological ill-health is far greater now that it was 50 years ago.

Life affects work and work affects life.
The statistics measuring the increases in sickness due to stress seem to reflect the dissatisfaction that people have with their lives generally. The issues that affect us outside work spill over into the work arena, and the stress we experience at work spills into the rest of our lives.

CHAPTER 2.
AIN'T NO SUNSHINE.

Psychological distress and depression.
Psychological distress comes in many forms and can be described by a whole range of negative emotions such as anger, anxiety, fear, sadness, stress or frustration. We experience psychological distress as part of our everyday lives and more often than not we are able to cope with 'feeling a bit down'. However, psychological distress is potentially damaging to us and if it persists unchecked for any length of time it can lead to depression, which is significantly more debilitating than just 'feeling a bit down'.

It is often said that depression is caused by a chemical imbalance in the brain. In many cases there is a reduction in the amount of certain neurotransmitters – monoamines such as serotonin and norepinephrine. However, regarding depression as just a chemical imbalance wildly misconstrues the disorder (1). The drop in norepinephrine and serotonin levels in the brain seems to be a result of over-arousal from negative introspection and lack of participation in activities that we enjoy doing. In simple terms, our heads become full of negative thoughts about our lives and ourselves, consequently we just can't face the effort of doing anything to cheer ourselves up.

The imbalance in chemicals is clearly implicated in depression, but both neurophysiological and psychological causes are implicated in depression. The US National Institute of Mental Health (2) points out that the influence of hormones in depression in women can also be found in pre-menstrual syndrome, menopause and post-natal depression. NIMH statistics state that, at some time in their lives, 20% of the women in the USA will suffer some form of depression that requires treatment. However, the NIMH also note that clearly not all women experiencing these abrupt hormonal shifts go on to develop depression. It seems to be women who are already vulnerable to depression because of other factors who experience the most negative effects. The NIMH found that the influence of genes plays an important role in vulnerability, and early life deprivation can lead to changes in brain function that increase susceptibility to depressive symptoms. Later in the book we will look at the effects of nature and nurture and people's susceptibility to psychological distress in more detail.

As I mentioned in the introduction, those who have never suffered from depression may not understand how debilitating it is when our neurotransmitters are causing the chemical imbalance in our brains. Often people who don't understand the problems of psychological distress are not terribly sympathetic to sufferers. In part this lack of sympathy is based on the idea that it's 'all in your mind'. As I noted earlier it's not as obvious as a broken leg and therefore any form of mental health problem can be perceived as somehow less real. It may appear that having a head full of negative thoughts is a straightforward problem. However, such is the power of the unconscious mind that once we become locked into this pattern of negative thinking it can suck us dry of any positive emotions and ultimately, in some tragic cases it robs people of the will to live.

I have worked with hundreds of clients with different problems, some everyday, some more unusual. Dave was experiencing a huge amount of stress over the deteriorating relationship with his wife and the worry of what would happen to him, his wife and their daughter if the marriage ended. Hilary was struggling to come to terms with the suicide of her teenage son. Louise was trying to block out the memories of the rapes committed on her by her husband of 20 years ago. Paula could not understand what was driving both her teenage daughters to self-harm. Harry was experiencing the guilt and sadness of his father's death in a nursing home, which had not lived up to its duty of care towards his dad and which Harry had not noticed. Cathy was still trying to block out the memories of childhood sexual abuse from a family member. Sarah was plagued by the memory of driving her car when a serious crash injured her granddaughter. Peter was simply worn down with an enormous workload and a boss who didn't seem to appreciate him. Mary had reached the age of 45 with no partner and no children, and her life had lost its sense of meaning. Lena's case was slightly different; she didn't appear to have a specific, tangible reason for feeling depressed. There was nothing obviously 'wrong' with Lena's life. On the contrary she had a lot to be thankful for but she just couldn't shake the general feeling of being down about life.

The effects of depression are both psychological and physiological. Psychological symptoms include a breadth of problems such as: feeling suicidal; the inability to concentrate on any task for very long; seemingly irrational fears; being unable to complete even simple tasks without making errors; experiencing disproportionately strong negative emotions such as anger or sadness in response to seemingly minor incidents; or even a numbness to any feeling at all. The physiological symptoms are just as varied: sleeplessness; loss of appetite; skin disorders; depletion of the immune system leading to increased susceptibility to infections; high blood pressure; even heart disease and cancer are implicated in the aetiology of psychological distress.

So, whilst depression may not appear to be a complex issue, the effects can be very harmful, and if unchecked they are potentially fatal. So let's try to explain how we can go from having negative introspective thoughts about our lives to the possibility of developing life threatening physiological and psychological symptoms.

The mind as a DVD library.
How do the negative thoughts manifest themselves? Well, my best explanation is that we have a library full of DVDs in our mind. Most psychologists believe in the theory of permanent memory. In other words everything we experience is stored away in our minds. However our recall system isn't very good and we struggle to recall memories at will. For example, as I write this in 2005 if you asked me what I was doing 30 years ago I would have to work out the date and then trawl my memory for what I was doing in 1975. But if I hear Bob Marley's song 'No Woman No Cry' it instantly brings back memories of what I was doing in college in that particular year when the song was constantly being played on the sound system

in the student union bar at my college. The DVD memories are all stacked in our mental library but sometimes we need a trigger, which can be either conscious or sub-conscious, in order to start playing a particular DVD memory. 'No Woman No Cry' is the trigger for me to start thinking of my student days.

In simple terms, some of the DVDs appear to be very positive memories, some appear very negative and many seem to be neutral. However, some DVD memories are a little bit more complicated because of the context within which we are viewing them. For example, Hilary (who I mentioned earlier) was trying to come to terms with the suicide of her teenage son. Some of Hilary's DVD memories of her son were positive memories, some were negative and sometimes a DVD memory would evoke both positive and negative feelings. She was viewing the DVD memories in the context of the death of her son, so they all had the potential to make her feel sad, but over time she was able to view these DVD memories in a more positive light.

When people are faced with personal challenges which they are finding difficulty coping with, they tend to play DVD memories that are predominantly negative, and they find it increasingly difficult to play either positive DVD memories or to see any positive aspects of the predominantly negative DVD memories. If, for example someone had just been made redundant from their job it would be quite understandable if they found themselves thinking mainly negative thoughts for a while. The negative DVD memories are evoked by the focus on the psychological distress the person is currently experiencing. Eventually these DVD memories become invasive thoughts that appear to come into the mind of the sufferer all the time and it becomes very hard for the person to stop these DVD memories from spinning around. This often occurs because the sufferer is unaware that some sub-conscious trigger has caused the negative DVD to start playing.

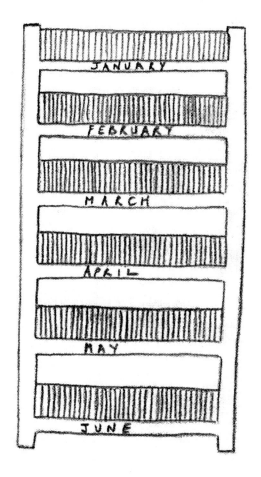

The Mind.
A library full of
DVDs, one recorded
for each day of
our lives.

Maureen's experience was an example of a subconscious trigger. Maureen had experienced a very stressful time at her previous place of work – a very busy accident and emergency department of a large hospital. She had eventually decided to leave and had been successful in applying for a job with the local authority housing group. However on her first day in the new job she experienced the negative DVD memories of her old job spinning around her head. This seemed to happen every morning, but the thoughts became less invasive as the day progressed. Eventually Maureen recognised what the sub-conscious trigger was for the negative DVD memories. The cleaners at the housing group used the same brand of floor cleaner as the hospital and the smell of the freshly cleaned floors sub-consciously evoked memories of the hospital.

The idea that we may have the ability to press the stop button for the DVD memory and eject it from our minds is a difficult concept to accept for many sufferers of depression. However, it is the continual playing of the invasive DVD memories that starts to affect the levels of the neurotransmitters in the brain and once this occurs, the depressive cycle is underway. As we will see later this can lead to negative 'memories' being created about the possible future outcome of an event. So when I use the word 'memory' in this book it can relate to both past events and future possible outcomes.

The reticular activating system – the brain's filter.
Our mind is a very complex piece of equipment. Psychologists admit that we still don't understand exactly how it works. What does seem clear is that our mind operates at both a conscious and sub-conscious level and between the two there is a cluster of brain cells, which acts as a filter - the reticular activating system (RAS). The filter allows certain information to go from the sub-conscious mind to the conscious mind depending on its relevance.

The sub-conscious mind is very powerful and can operate in what appears to be an almost mystical way. In the 1950s Juan Fangio the Argentinean racing driver dominated the sport of motor racing and was world champion for many years. On one occasion he was racing at a particular circuit that had a blind left-hand bend. As Fangio approached the bend he began to brake gently to allow himself to negotiate the bend at the correct speed. However, he found himself almost unable to take his foot off the brake pedal. For some reason he braked far harder and much longer than he normally would have done for a bend of this magnitude. As he rounded the bend he saw that there had been a crash involving several other cars, which, had he not slowed down considerably, he would have smashed straight into.

Due to his actions he was able to negotiate his way safely around the crash and go on to win the race.

Commentators on the sport marvelled at what they described as Fangio's sixth sense, his uncanny ability to somehow anticipate the accident. However, Fangio himself was quite perturbed at what had occurred because he couldn't understand what it was that had made him brake so much harder than he would normally have done. He was worried that if he found himself in similar circumstances again he might not be able to 'sense' his way out of danger a second time.

A few months later he woke up one morning with the answer. He realised what it was that his sub-conscious mind had picked up which had lead him to brake uncharacteristically hard. As he was driving along the straight approaching the left-hand bend the main grandstand with all the spectators was located on his right at the junction of the bend. Fangio was the world champion and was used to seeing all the spectators' heads inclined at an angle to watch him drive down the straight. In other words all the spectators would be looking to their left to see him drive down the straight towards the bend. However, his sub-conscious mind picked up the fact that the mosaic effect of all those spectators' heads looking down the track towards Fangio's car was not present. The pattern of spectator gaze was such that Fangio was being ignored; their attention was drawn to something on the other side of the bend, which they could see from their position high up in the grandstand, but Fangio could not see from his position low down on the track. Once Fangio had realised what it was that had made him brake so hard he was then able to factor this information into his conscious mind in the future whenever he raced at circuits with a blind bend.

Previously Fangio's sub-conscious mind had been aware of the gazing pattern of spectators' heads but it had never been particularly relevant to the situation and therefore the information remained in his subconscious unable to get through the filter. Because of the importance of the changes in gaze pattern that his sub-conscious mind recognised, the information was communicated at a *sub-conscious* level to his feet when he began to brake. Until Fangio could identify *consciously* what it was that made him brake harder it was leaving it to chance as to whether his subconscious mind would do the same thing in similar circumstances again.

It's no coincidence that he got the answer immediately on waking up. When we dream we are in a state of sleep characterised by rapid eye movement (REM) and during this state we seem to be more in tune with our sub-conscious mind. Fangio's alarm clock probably went off whilst he was dreaming about this particular incident prompting the answer to suddenly came into his conscious mind.

The filter operates in much the same way for people experiencing psychological distress – they don't 'see' the positive things in their lives, despite the fact that the positive things are there. Their filters allow the negative experiences into the conscious mind and keep the positive experiences submerged in the sub-conscious. The filter also seems to operate with our other senses. For example I was explaining the filters to a friend of mine over a coffee at a busy pavement café in Spain. As we were talking I noticed she was listening intently to my explanation but I could see over her shoulder a mother and baby at the next table. The baby had been crying moments earlier and the mother had got up and rocked it back to sleep. I asked my friend whether she had heard the sound of a baby crying several moments ago. My friend paused for a moment and said "Yes, but I hadn't noticed it until you mentioned it". The sound had remained in her sub-conscious only passing through the filter when I drew her attention to it.

To explain this to my clients I give them the following exercise. I ask them to make a mental note of how many red cars they see on the journey home from their appointment. The next time I see them I ask them to tell me how many silver cars they noticed on the journey home. I usually get a very blank look and a confused explanation of how they had not been aware of any silver cars because their focus had been on red cars. However, they always concede that there must have been silver cars present on their journey home because in England it's the most common colour for cars. Of course they 'saw' the silver cars otherwise they would have crashed into one of them! The silver cars didn't register on their conscious mind because the filter was only allowing red cars into their conscious mind. It's the same when we are experiencing some kind of psychological distress; the filter allows things that are related to our distress into the conscious mind because they seem more significant.

If the filters are set to allow the negative DVD memories of our lives into our conscious mind then inevitably they increase our levels of self-doubt. If the filter only allows through DVDs showing past difficulties and the potential threats and dangers in a situation that could result in our failure, then self-doubt begins to creep into our minds and destroys our confidence.

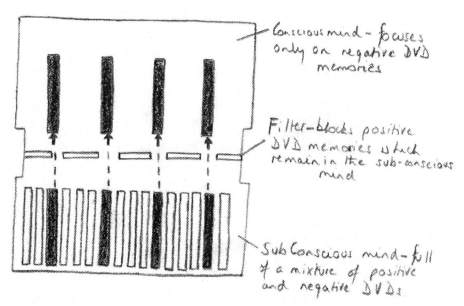

Conscious mind - focuses only on negative DVD memories

Filter - blocks positive DVD memories which remain in the sub-conscious mind

Sub Conscious mind - full of a mixture of positive and negative DVDs

Here's a little story that shows how the filters work in practice to cause doubt to creep into a situation. After my divorce I eventually ended up buying a house in the next village to my ex-wife, Rebecca. Initially I had great difficulty buying a house in that location because it was a very popular village and it was also in the middle of a boom in the housing market. Eventually I managed to buy a house previously owned by Rebecca's Aunt Sybil who had died a couple of years previously.

Sybil had been a very keen gardener and in the middle of the back garden she had a beautiful wrought iron water pump and a large stone trough which formed a very attractive feature. The garden had become very overgrown since Sybil's death and I decided I would clear all the shrubs and trees, take up the lawn and replace it with stone chippings and earthenware pots with plants. I was fortunate that a very kind girlfriend, Kim who I had recently started a relationship with, offered to give me a hand to clear the garden. I mentioned that I was going to give the trough and water pump to Rebecca as a reminder of her Aunt Sybil. Kim was quite surprised and remarked at how expensive these features would be to replace. I said that I felt it would be a kind gesture to give them to Rebecca, as she had been very fond of her Aunt Sybil.

At this Kim became very quiet and I sensed that she was quite troubled about the apparent strong connection to my ex-wife which the water pump seemed to symbolise. I tried to convince her that she was probably reading more into the gesture than it merited and eventually she seemed reassured. Later that day we decided to go for a walk around the village in the late evening sunshine, which was something we had done quite often. After our walk we decided to stop off in one of the village pubs for a drink. As we were enjoying a couple of beers Kim suddenly said to me "Do you know how many black iron water pumps there are in this village?" She then laughed and proceeded to tell me the location of about seven or eight water pumps dotted in various gardens throughout the village. Despite the fact that the walk we had just been on was quite familiar to her, she had never noticed the water pumps. They had remained in her sub-conscious mind. However, because Sybil's water pump represented something negative that troubled her, her filters were activated to consciously notice all the water pumps in the village.

People who are experiencing psychological distress have their filters set to notice the negative things in their lives and consequently that's what they see and hear. Of course the negative things are there, but so are positive things it's just that the good things remain in the background of the sub-conscious mind - they just don't have the same level of significance. The more we filter out the positive DVD memories and filter in the negative DVD memories then the greater our levels of self-doubt.

The curse of self-doubt.
The continual playing of the negative DVD memories begins to lead to self-doubt and the belief that we are to blame for what has happened to us. We then start to feel that we are inadequate to deal with the situation, that we should have done something different or even that we should have been somebody different. With almost all the people I work with self-doubt features very highly. Sarah believed she could have avoided the accident in which her granddaughter was injured, (despite the insurance company's view to the contrary) and she completely lost her confidence to drive. Harry's guilt over his apparent failure to notice the inadequate care provided by the nursing home for his father was compounded by the fact that he was himself a nurse. He subsequently lost confidence in his ability to diagnose even simple ailments at work. Even Louise who was raped quite violently felt that she was somehow to blame for allowing this to happen to her.

Self-doubt leads to a lack of confidence, so offering someone suffering from depression the advice to "pull yourself together" is at best unhelpful and at worst it simply reinforces the self-doubt they are already experiencing.

The greater the self-doubt, the more depressed the sufferers' mood becomes. The more depressed they are then the less inclined they feel to take part in activities that previously gave them any pleasure. The less they take part in any enjoyable activities then the recent memories for each day are more likely to be labelled as sad, negative DVD memories and are stored as such in the library. And so the cycle continues. Even if positive, happy experiences have featured in the sufferers' day they are filtered out, so when the DVD memory is recalled at the end of the day it is perceived as another depressing episode in the life of the sufferer. Ultimately this leads the sufferer to experience increasingly low levels of self-esteem

Summary of Chapter 2. Ain't no sunshine.

Psychological distress and depression? Psychological distress has many forms – anxiety, fear, stress and perhaps the most common form, depression. Depression is the result of a combination of a focus on negative introspective thoughts and a lack of participation in pleasure giving activities. The negative thoughts can emanate from a whole variety of different problems we may face in our lives. Over a period of time, if we continually have negative thoughts, it can cause a decrease in the levels of the neurotransmitters nor-epinephrine and serotonin in the brain. These neurotransmitters are associated with feelings of well being.

The mind as a DVD library. When we are depressed we sub-consciously start to do two things. Firstly we play the predominantly negative DVD memories from the past. Secondly we find it increasingly difficult to focus on the positive aspects of any of our DVD memories.

The reticular activating system – the brain's filter. The reason we find ourselves focussing on negative DVD memories is because the RAS filter draws our conscious mind to anything linked to the psychological distress we are suffering. The filter allows negative DVDs from our subconscious into our conscious mind. The filter makes sure the positive DVDs are left in our subconscious mind and they go relatively unnoticed.

The curse of self-doubt. The negative DVD memories contain images of ourselves in the situations where we are struggling to cope and this causes us to doubt our ability to handle the situation successfully. In turn this starts to negatively impact our self-esteem.

CHAPTER 3.
BELIEVING IS SEEING.

As we mentioned in the previous chapter, the filter doesn't allow us to see things in a balanced way. Instead, the recent past and the present are full of negative DVDs. After a while, depressed people can find that the filter works so effectively with memories of the past that it starts to operate in the same way when it comes to playing DVDs about what the future might look like.

Self-fulfilling prophecy – if you believe it's going to be a disaster, you're probably right.
The power of the sub-conscious mind can begin to significantly affect our psychological well being in a very negative way. The filters have now been set to notice anything that is potentially dangerous or threatening in both a physical and psychological sense. So when a depressed person imagines what might happen in a certain situation in the future they start to see all the potential pitfalls - the self-doubt once again creeps in. The more they visualise a future event where things could perceivably go wrong, then the more likely it is that this will be the final outcome. The net effect of this negative visualisation is that it increases our levels of self-doubt to the point where we unconsciously self-sabotage our efforts without even realising.

The subtle interplay between the DVD memories of the past and the DVDs we are creating about possible futures is often seen in sports psychology, which offers some very rich insights into the concept of self-fulfilling prophecy.

In the Euro 2004 soccer tournament England played Portugal, the host nation, in the quarterfinal stage of the tournament. The score at the end of the match was 1-1 and the match had to be decided in a penalty shoot out.

David Beckham, the England Captain, was due to take the first penalty for England. He waited nervously to take the penalty against a background of Portuguese fans loudly willing him to miss. The pressure in the shoot out was enormous – success meant progression to the semi-finals, failure meant the early plane home. Beckham ran up to the penalty spot, struck the ball and watched it sail hopelessly over the bar and into the gleeful Portuguese fans.

So what was going on in Beckham's head as he ran up to take the penalty? A few days earlier in the group stage of the tournament England were playing France. The English were already winning 1-0 when they were awarded a penalty half way through the second half of the match. If the penalty was scored and a 2-0 advantage taken then victory was virtually assured. Beckham stepped up to take the penalty and clipped it to the goalkeeper's right. The goalkeeper dived athletically and saved the shot. England went on to lose that game 2-1.

Who knows what was going on in Beckham's mind when he ran up to take the penalty against Portugal in the shoot out? However, if his filter was filtering in the DVD memory of his failure to score the penalty against France then the self-doubt may have started to creep into his conscious mind and consequently, he may have started to sub-consciously visualise himself missing the penalty against Portugal - a self-fulfilling prophecy.

Whilst we can't be certain what was going on in David Beckham's mind, here is another example of self-fulfilling prophecy which seems a lot clearer. I was once asked to give a motivational talk to a group of thirty highflying people in a multi-national IT company. I was told I could talk on any subject I wanted as long as it would: a) make people think; b) be quite uplifting; c) have some relevance to the world of work. So I decided to see if I could investigate further the power of the filter in creating negative self-fulfilling prophecies.

I turned up to the venue early and laid the tables out so that each table could accommodate seven people. I had previously asked the organiser to ensure that on each table we had six highfliers and a senior manager who would be there to observe the day and to allow the highfliers an opportunity to network with the senior managers throughout the day. On each table I placed a plate, a cereal bowl, a bag of flour, a potato masher, a knife and a small coin. When everyone was seated I explained that I was a psychologist and that I wanted everyone to take part in an experiment. The reaction was very varied - amusement, interest, discomfort and negativity were registered on the faces of various members of the group.

I then proceeded to demonstrate how the experiment would operate. I explained that the senior manager on each table would be the organiser of the experiment. They would pour the flour into the cereal bowl and pack it quite tightly with the potato masher. They would then turn it upside down like a sandcastle to produce a flour pie on the plate. On top of the flour pie they would place the coin.

Each of the six highfliers would then take it in turns to cut away a slice of the flour pie. The flour pie would then gradually become more and more narrow and increasingly less stable. Eventually one person would inevitably start to cut a small slice of the flour pie and the coin would topple off the top of the flour pie. The forfeit for failure was that the person who was making the cut when this occurred would have to pick the coin out of the flour using their teeth and thereby getting their face covered in flour.

I explained that on each table we would run the experiment three times and on each occasion that a participant knocked over the coin they would be removed from the game for the next round. Although I was careful not to verbalise this to the group, in effect, each table of six highfliers would eventually be left with three winners and three losers with flour on their faces!

Having explained the rules of the experiment there was again a range of different reactions from the group. I reinforced the importance of making sure the rules of the experiment were adhered to strictly. The rules stated that on each cut of the knife it should be a continuous movement from the top of the flour pie all the way to the tray. The senior manager on each table was to be the adjudicator and would make anyone who did not adhere to the rules take another cut.

After this I asked all the high fliers to privately jot down on a piece of paper their answers to the following questions:

1. On a scale of 1 – 10 how appropriate did they feel this experiment was to a group of highfliers in a blue chip IT company, with 1 being 'very inappropriate' and 10 being 'very appropriate'.
2. On a scale of 1 –10 how well did they think they would perform on this task, with 1 being 'not very well' and 10 being 'very well'.
3. On a scale of 1 – 10 how did they feel about getting flour on their faces, with 1 being 'very uncomfortable about the prospect' and 10 being 'very unconcerned about the prospect'.

The high fliers were than asked to put the piece of paper with their answers in their pockets until the end of the experiment. I emphasised the importance of everyone being absolutely honest about their feelings and reassured them that their individual identity would not be linked to the answers they had written. We then proceeded to conduct three rounds of the experiment and eventually on each table we ended up with three winners and three losers.

I asked everyone to take the piece of paper with their answers out of their pockets and if they had ended up with flour on their faces they were asked to write an "L" on their paper signifying they had been a Loser. If they had evaded the indignity of getting flour on their faces they were asked to write a "W" on their paper for Winner. The senior managers then collected the papers in and were instructed to sort the papers into two groups – Winners Vs Losers. They then tallied up the scores for each group and calculated the average score for each question for Winners Vs Losers.

For question 1, how appropriate was the activity, the Winners were significantly more positive about the activity than the Losers.

For question 2, how well did people think they would perform, the Winners were slightly more confident of performing well than the Losers.

For question 3, how did people feel about the prospect of getting flour on their face, the Losers were very significantly more concerned about getting flour on their faces than the Winners.

In simple terms it seemed that the more worried people were about the threat of getting flour on their faces, then the more likely they were to get flour on their faces. The psychological worry translated itself into less confident cuts with the knife. The more tense people were when cutting the flour pie the more likely they were to dislodge the coin and consequently get flour on their faces by completing the forfeit of picking the coin up with their teeth.

So, the moral of the story is that if we fear a negative outcome we often contribute to increasing the likelihood of that negative outcome actually coming to fruition. If our filter is set to spot all the potential negative outcomes in a given situation, it's almost as if the brain runs a programme about the potential negative outcome and the body then automatically works to deliver the programme accurately – we literally set ourselves up to fail.

Thinking errors.

One of the main difficulties in combating any kind of psychological distress and especially depression is trying to re-set the filter so that it reverses the process i.e. it filters in the positive DVD memories and filters out the negative ones.

It's quite difficult to do this particularly when we are experiencing high levels of self-doubt. So what is it that keeps the filter in place so that the negative memories of the past slip into our conscious minds? The answer is that we make what are known as 'thinking errors'.

Thinking errors are sub-conscious negative assumptions we make about our world which when challenged often prove to be unfounded. David Burns (1) identified some examples of common Thinking Errors.

1. All or Nothing Thinking. Things are perceived in black or white categories. Anything short of perfection is viewed as a failure.

2. Over Generalisation. A single negative event is perceived as a never-ending pattern of defeat. The word "always" is often used to describe negative events and "never" to describe positive events.

3. Mental Filter. Negative events are dwelt on to the exclusion of any positive events. This is described as the drop of ink that discolours the entire glass of water.

4. Disqualifying the Positives. Positive experiences are described as not counting - it was easy, anyone can do that.

5. Jumping to Conclusions. Negative interpretations occur even though there are no facts to support the conclusion - everyone's got it in for me today.

6. Magnification and Minimisation. Magnifying your own errors or other people's achievements. Minimising your own achievements or other people's errors.

7. Emotional Reason. Assuming that your negative emotions reflect the way things really are.

8. Should Statements. When directed at you they encourage failure or defeat. When directed at others they encourage anger, frustration and resentment.

9. Labelling and Mislabelling. An extreme form of generalisation. Instead of describing an error you attach a negative label to yourself or others - I'm hopeless. She is an idiot. The language is often highly coloured or emotionally loaded.

10. Personalisation. Seeing yourself or someone else as the cause of some negative external event which the individual was not responsible for.

David Burns did a wonderful job of identifying these errors. There seems to be a lot of overlap between his third error – Mental Filter and my theory of how the RAS filter works. However, I believe that it's the third error that is the key, the rest of the thinking errors seem to operate in a way that they keep the mental filter in place. So, for example, with all or nothing thinking it is the error itself that only allows the negative aspect of a DVD memory into the person's mind.

A simple example of this is Danny the MD of a corporate clothing company. He spent an enormous amount of time trying to win a contract to supply staff uniforms to a chain of leisure clubs. Danny's company was shortlisted down to one of just two candidates, from an initial list of eight companies who had submitted proposals. Eventually the leisure company chose Danny's competitor. Danny was deeply disappointed and took absolutely no comfort from the fact that his company had come second. It was a classic example of all or nothing thinking. The thinking error was causing the negative DVD memories to get through the filter. He could not see any positive DVD memories from the bidding process, despite the fact that they were there. This error resulted in only negative DVD memories making it through the filter into Danny's conscious mind.

After I talked it through with Danny, he decided that one of the positive DVD memories was the close relationship he had built with one of the directors of the leisure company. Danny decided to keep in close contact with this director over the next few months to see how well his competitor was doing. Two months later Danny found out that his competitor was having difficulty in supplying one of the uniform items. The leisure company, through Danny's friendly director, consequently approached Danny to ask him to supply this particular item of uniform which proved very profitable for Danny's company.

I have also come across some graphic examples of people making multiple thinking errors through my counselling experience. Earlier in the book, I mentioned Paula a woman in her early forties who had two teenage daughters who were both self-harming. For no apparent reason they would both inflict cuts on their arms. Paula simply could not understand why they were doing this and despite the best efforts of herself and her husband the two girls refused to give any reasons for their behaviour except to say that it had nothing to do with their parents.

In Paula's own words. "I just can't understand it. The two of them are so stupid. They have everything they need: a nice house, loving parents, a decent standard of living. They're doing well academically; they have lovely friends. I feel like a complete failure. Other parents don't have this type of problem with their children. These days they never seem to be happy about anything. Take Christmas day for example, we were just sitting down to watch the film in the evening when they ruined the whole day with their behaviour by starting an argument for no reason at all. Half an hour later when I went to my younger daughter's bedroom I found she had cut herself again."

Poor Paula was understandably very worried and depressed about the situation with her daughters whom she clearly loved very much. When I went back over what Paula had said to me, we started to unpick the thinking errors.

Paula recognised that her daughters weren't stupid. In fact, both of them were very bright young women. Paula was mislabelling them with her frustrations and by telling them they were stupid was only inflaming the situation. Paula rephrased her statement to reflect her view that their choice of behaviour appeared to be very destructive and without any apparent logic to it.

Paula had then described herself as a complete failure, which may have been another example of mislabelling, but was also an example of all or nothing thinking. When we talked about her role in parenting the girls over the years it became clear that the self-harm was relatively recent and that Paula had been very successful in many aspects of parenting.

Paula's view that other parents didn't have this type of problem is also another thinking error. She may not know any parents who have similar problems but they certainly exist. Most teenagers go through a difficult patch and some choose extreme forms of behaviour during this difficult time in their lives.

"The children never seem to be happy about anything." Paula recognised herself that this was an over generalisation and that there were a number of things they did take pleasure from.

Finally Paula had, quite understandably, allowed the fact that her younger daughter had cut herself to colour the whole of Christmas day. On further examination Christmas day had, on the whole, been a pretty positive experience for the family. Whilst her younger daughter had inflicted a minor cut to her arm, the whole day had not been the disaster it seemed. However, it was the multiple thinking errors that had kept the filter in place so that only the negative DVDs made it into Paula's conscious mind.

The thinking errors that Paula was making increased her feelings of self-doubt and failure and this was in turn leading to a feeling of helplessness about her ability to control the outcome of her daughters' behaviour. She began to recognise that her focus on negative DVD memories, (both past and future memories), was leading to self-fulfilling prophecy because her depressed feelings had the potential to increase the arguments and rows which often preceded the incidences of self-harming by her daughters.

There was one point in our conversation where Paula was able to laugh at an obvious irony. Paula's filters had been set to notice every time there was an argument with one of her daughters. One day she articulated this thinking error to her daughters. She told them, in no uncertain terms that they were 'always' arguing. At which point her daughters began to argue vehemently that this was not the case, which in turn Paula used against them to reinforce the thinking error. "See, there you go again, always arguing!" The self-fulfilling prophecy had come home to roost.

She had filtered out the positive conversations with her daughters because they were not potentially threatening. The positive conversations went unnoticed by her filters. They 'didn't count' because when her daughters were in a positive frame of mind they didn't self-harm. By not challenging this thinking error she allowed the filter to draw attention to DVDs of her daughters 'always' arguing. By doing this Paula had actually created an argument with them, thereby increasing the likelihood of them self-harming - self-fulfilling prophecy.

It doesn't mean that Paula was responsible for her daughters' self-harming behaviour. That was clearly their choice. However, by challenging her thinking errors Paula filtered in positive aspects of her daughters' behaviour and consequently felt more positive about them. This meant she was able to deal with their poor choice of self-harming behaviour in a calmer manner, which reduced the likelihood of arguments and the consequent self-harming. Later in the book I'll talk more about the concept of 'choices and consequences', and how it can be linked to thinking errors.

Summary of Chapter 3. Believing is seeing.

Self-fulfilling prophecy. The cycle of repeatedly playing negative DVDs of past events where we judged ourselves as failures begins to impact on the outcome of how we will handle similar situations in the future. We believe that we will fail in the future because we have lots of negative DVD evidence to show us how we failed in the past. We then create negative DVD memories about the possible failures in the future. Sports psychology provides plenty of examples of the relationship between negative expectation and failure.

Thinking errors. These are the negative assumptions and conclusions that we draw about others and ourselves. Thinking errors keep the filter firmly in place. They make sure that we focus on negative DVD memories. The negative DVD memories are filtered from the sub-conscious into the conscious mind. The positive DVD memories are left in the sub-conscious mind and don't register in the conscious mind. As a result of the thinking errors fixing the filter in place, the cycle of self-doubt, lack of confidence, low self esteem and negative self-fulfilling prophecies occur. With the result that with the consequent failure yet another negative DVD is stored in the mind's library ready to be registered on the conscious mind when it is pushed through the filter.

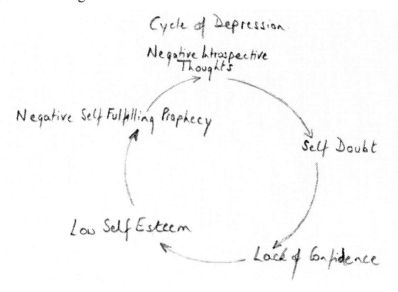

CHAPTER 4
INTO EVERY LIFE A LITTLE RAIN MUST FALL.

Life Events.

Rich or poor, black or white, gay or straight, whoever we are, it is inevitable that we will all experience what are known as 'life events' at some point during our lives. Life events include situations that are clearly negative such as the death of a close relative, a relationship breaking down or being made redundant from our job. Equally, even potentially happy events such as the birth of a child or moving house can also be quite stressful. The natural course of life brings us into contact with events that can be psychologically challenging. The affect of life events can mean increasing amounts of psychological distress on the part of the person going through the life event. This is inevitable - into every life a little rain must fall.

As I mentioned earlier in the book, the symptoms we experience when going through a difficult time may be both psychological, such as anxiety, stress and depression; or they could be related to various physical ailments. Life events are the external triggers that can cause us to suffer psychological distress. They have the power to set in train the cycle of thinking errors - the filter - negative DVDs - self-doubt – low self-esteem - self-fulfilling prophecy. If the thinking errors remain unchallenged the cycle remains unbroken and the consequence is the chemical imbalance in the brain that is diagnosed as depression.

I've worked with many people who were experiencing depression as a result of having gone through some difficult life events. In these instances it is relatively easy to pinpoint the source of the depression – take Stan, for example. A man in his mid forties trying to come to terms with impending blindness as a result of his diabetic condition. It's not hard to understand why he might be feeling depressed. This type of depression is known as exogenous depression - there is a fairly obvious external cause of the depression.

However, I've also worked with many people who don't know why they are experiencing a range of psychologically distressing emotions. Lena was fairly typical in her response to this predicament. She had a good job, two lovely children, a caring husband and a beautiful house. There was nothing obvious about her depression, no clear external cause that she could pinpoint. In a sense this made her feel even worse because she felt guilty about being depressed for the very reason that she didn't appear to have anything in her life to be depressed about. Her depression is described as endogenous – there is no obvious external 'rainfall' to point to as the cause for her depression.

All of us experience life events but not everyone succumbs to the depressive cycle. On the other hand, some people succumb to depression but don't appear to have any life events to deal with. So why some people and not others? The answer lies internally, in our psychological make-up. It is the interaction between our internal psychological make-up and our external world, which defines how well we will deal with life. My explanation for this is pegs and holes. Imagine there is round hole in the side of a bathtub full of water. If we put a square peg in the hole in an attempt to prevent the water escaping then the water will seep through because the peg doesn't fit the hole.

Each one of us is unique. We are pegs who are all a slightly different shape to each other, and no two pegs are exactly the same. People's internal psychological make-up makes them the peg shape that they are. This may help them deal with certain aspects of their life very well but may not help them deal so effectively with other challenges in their lives. It helps explain why some people may be more prone to psychological distress than others.

In order to understand how our internal psychological make-up interacts with our external world we need a model to work with. The Human Factors model below attempts to explain how we become the people we are.

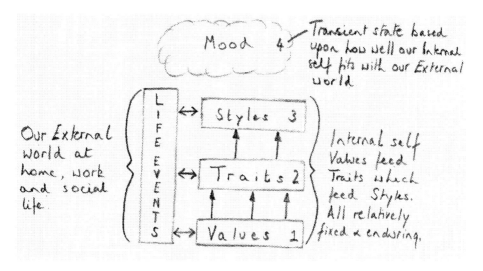

Mood 4 — Transient state based upon how well our Internal self fits with our External world

L
I
F
E
E
V
E
N
T
S

Styles 3

Traits 2

Values 1

Our External world at home, work and social life.

Internal self Values feed Traits which feed Styles. All relatively fixed & enduring.

Values.

The base on which our being is built is at level 1 in the Human Factors model, our Values. These are the beliefs we have about the world and those around us. Our values give us a code of acceptable conduct about how we should interact with individual people and society as a whole. Our values are represented in the attitudes and behaviours that we strongly embrace, as opposed to the attitudes and behaviours, which we eschew.

Where do we get our values? Usually it's a combination of nature and nurture. We inherit some of them directly through our parents, and some of them from the effect of the environment we are exposed to during our formative years. Our values are continually being developed but by the time we reach our mid to late twenties it seems that they become relatively fixed and enduring. Our values don't change much unless, like St Paul on his way to Damascus, we are hit by a bolt of lightening which fundamentally shakes our values and leads us to question them.

Our behaviour is based on the fundamental values we hold. In particular, those values which we hold most dear are the ones which are likely to have the most significant impact on our behaviour and are the ones which are least likely to be influenced by the effects of different situations. For example, Kelly is a woman who was brought up to believe very strongly that we should always tell the truth regardless of the situation we are in. In some circumstances this is very desirable. Kelly had found out that her friend's husband had been unfaithful. Kelly's belief was that her friend needed to know the brutal truth so that she could deal with it. Another person, Alison, who also knew about this, felt that it was not their place to give the mutual friend this information. Kelly always speaks her mind regardless of the situation. Whether it's about a friend's husband having an affair or being asked her opinion about the expensive new dress someone has just bought. It's one of Kelly's fundamental values.

Traits.
At the next level up, in the Human Factors model, we have Traits. These include for example: personality traits such as introversion/extroversion; strength traits (1) which are about the things we have a natural talent for, such as the ability to think analytically or the ability to bring harmony to a situation; our motivational traits – such as whether we are motivated by the promise of something good if we do it, or the threat of something bad if we don't. (2). There are various different forms of traits and they interact with, and influence each other. The key thing about traits is that they are the tangible manifestations (demonstrated in the way we act and talk) of the internal values we hold dear.

Once again, the traits become relatively fixed and enduring by the time we reach our mid to late twenties. There are many different psychometric tests that measure lots of different personality traits such as introversion/extroversion. The traits are bi-polar constructs, which means that the two ends of the construct are opposite to each other. Psychometric tests measure our responses against the general population and produce normal distribution curves

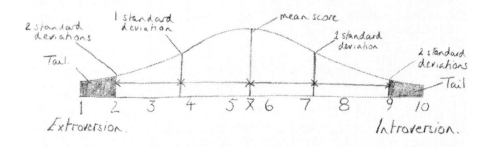

About 80% of people fall within 2 standard deviations of the mean score (the average) so they are unlikely to be extreme in their traits for most personality constructs. So, in the distribution curve above if we have someone whose test score is 4 for introversion/extroversion this puts them on the extrovert side of the average score but not in the extreme 'tail' for extroversion. This person will tend to be outgoing in company and may be livelier in their behaviour then someone who tends towards introversion. However, if they are attending a funeral for example, they will be able to modify their behaviour based on the situation. A colleague of mine Craig is an extreme extrovert whose score of 2 places him in the tail end of the scale. At a funeral Craig finds it hard not to tell funny stories about the deceased. Some people may be offended by Craig's behaviour, believing that it is inappropriate and disrespectful. At a funeral Craig is a square peg in a round hole. However, when Craig is attending a party he's perceived in a very positive light because telling jokes and funny stories are seen as desirable behaviours – he's a square peg in a square hole.

On a psychometric test that measures 16 different personality traits most people have scores in the tail end on about four traits. The more traits a person has in the tail ends then the less likely a situation is to influence their behaviour, and the more extreme their personality is likely to be.

Style.
The next level in the Human Factors model is described as Style. Based on the two previous levels we develop a certain style in terms of the way we typically behave in certain situations. Style is the tangible manifestation of our Traits and Values. There are many measures of different styles, such as management style (the way we typically manage people), or conflict style (the way we typically try to deal with conflict).

Styles are defined by words that describe the behaviour of individuals in certain situations. For example, one woman I worked with who was in her 60s, Angela, was described as having an "authoritarian" management style. Listening to Angela it was easy to picture her barking out orders to her subordinate colleagues. Angela believed that this was the only way to get people to do the job to her high standards. She told me that she had been sent on a management course to try to help her change her style to become more democratic, but she found it very hard to change her ways. She was very happy to deal with conflict in a direct fashion, which was a pronounced aspect of her personality. In one conversation I asked her how appropriate it was to give someone a public 'rollicking' if they had made a careless error. She paused and shook her head slowly "Maybe I'm just an old fashioned person but I honestly believe that if someone has made a careless mistake they should be told in no uncertain terms about it – then maybe they'll be more careful next time." Angela's values in this situation manifested themselves in her trait for dealing with conflict very directly, which was in turn, reflected in her authoritarian style. Once again, as with Values and Traits, Style is pretty fixed and enduring: once we reach a certain age we don't change much.

Mood.
At the next level we've got Mood. Here, the difference between level 4 and the preceding levels is that mood isn't fixed. Sometimes we're happy, sometimes, we're sad and this is likely to be influenced by the external situation we find ourselves in. For most of us, the more a situation suits our values, traits and styles, then the more positive our mood is likely to be – a square peg in a square hole. The less we are suited to the situations i.e. the more challenged we are, then the greater the potential for anxiety, stress and depression. Certain external situations, such as the death of a loved one, would typically affect most people negatively to some degree. But other external situations only affect us negatively if they clash with our values, traits and style. Some people enjoy dealing with conflict whilst other people hate it. As the old proverb says "one man's meat is another man's poison."

I spent some time working with John who was experiencing a lot of stress in the new job to which he had recently been promoted. This was a life event that should have been a very positive event for John who had worked hard for this promotion. However, in the cut and thrust world of John's industry he had become the most junior person on a management team where the culture in meetings encouraged the managers to be openly critical of each other if things were not going well. John found this blunt, and sometimes bruising environment, very difficult to work in. When he was growing up John had come from a family where the value of respecting your elders had been reinforced. It was not deemed acceptable to be openly critical of other people in such an overt manner. This value had translated into certain traits within John. He tended towards introversion and one of his strengths was harmony. He naturally wanted to keep the peace with others, rather than 'falling out with people', which was how he perceived the situation in management meetings. John's style in terms of conflict management tended towards 'accommodating'. In other words, it was a style, which was high on co-operation with others but quite low on assertiveness.

In meetings, John's boss, Paul, was of the view that "We're all big lads who can take it on the chin and dish it out in equal measure if there are problems with the business." Consequently, after a few months of working in this environment, John began to feel very uncomfortable and was aware that Paul was beginning to form a negative view of his ability to participate effectively in management meetings.

John's values had influenced his traits, which had, in turn influenced his natural style. Unfortunately John's style was deemed to be inappropriate in the management meetings. This left John experiencing high stress levels. John was a square peg in a round hole. John was starting to filter the negative DVD memories of management meetings into his mind. He doubted his ability to operate effectively in meetings and there was a danger that self-fulfilling prophecies were coming to fruition because of the thinking errors he was making. "I never seem to say the right things in the meetings." "The whole meeting was a disaster from start to finish."

John was able to solve his difficulties by accepting that he wasn't like the other senior managers in the meeting because of his different values. He was able to operate effectively in these meetings provided that he didn't feel he was compromising his values. John was fortunate that he had a good background in finance and was very strong with figures and data. By thoroughly preparing for the meetings he could let the figures do the talking and was able to utilise the data to draw conclusions in a less personal way. So rather than berate the Sales Director for not achieving his targets as other senior managers might, John would use the data to ask the Sales Director some very polite but pertinent questions. "I notice from the figures that the average value of a contract sold this month seems to have fallen by 25% from the same month last year. What are the underlying reasons for this, and what plans are there in place to rectify it?" This approach matched John's values, but also reassured his boss Paul that he was able to participate effectively in meetings.

Our mood is dictated by the relationship between our internal psychological make up (the Human Factors) and our external world (Life Events). We all have to deal with challenging life events, but some people find them relatively easy to deal with. Those who find it difficult are more prone to psychological distress, as we will see later.

Summary of Chapter 4. Into every life a little rain must fall.

Life events. These are the significant milestone events that mark our lives. They can be either positive (moving to a new house or the birth of a child) or negative (the death of a close relative or the break up of a relationship) but both have the power to induce a certain amount of distress in us. Depression emanating from these is described as exogenous i.e. there is a fairly obvious cause. Depression where there is no obvious external cause is described as endogenous.

The Human Factors Model.
Values. These are the beliefs that we inherit from the effects of both nature and nurture. They tend to be relatively fixed and enduring. They don't change much by the time we reach a certain age - probably our mid to late 20s. They are the bedrock upon which most of our observable behaviour is built.

Traits. These develop throughout our formative years and, like values, seem to be relatively fixed and enduring, although they are influenced to a degree by the situation we find ourselves in. Traits can be measured against population norms and the traits which are most pronounced, compared against the rest of the population, are the ones which will be least affected by the situation.

Styles. These are the tangible summation of our values and traits. We can describe a person's style from what we see and hear. We can usually work out some of the traits and values that underpin a person's style. Because styles are based on values and traits, once again they tend to be relatively fixed and enduring. Style demonstrates how we typically interact with our external world

Mood. Moods are transient; they change according to how well we feel we are equipped to cope with what's going on in our external world. If our external world is not a good fit with our internal world then our mood can become depressed. It's important to remember that even clinically depressed people are not depressed all the time – mood is transient, it changes.

CHAPTER 5.
SELF-KNOWLEDGE.

In Greek history legend has it that when the ancient Greeks wanted some advice when faced with difficult decisions they would consult the Oracle of Apollo at Delphi for the answer. On the wall of the Oracle was written, "From the gods comes the saying, know thyself."

Self knowledge is a very important concept, particularly as the conclusion that most psychologists draw is that once we reach a certain age we don't change fundamentally. In the previous chapter we looked at what makes us who we are in terms of our values, traits and styles and how we interact with the external world. This chapter looks at the consequence of having certain values, traits and styles in relation to psychological distress. It will also look more closely at the interplay between our internal world (the values, traits and styles) and the external situations that evoke strong emotional reactions – life events.

Are some people more prone to psychological distress than others?

A client called Sally once asked me whether some people had values, traits and styles which made them more likely to suffer from stress, anxiety and depression. Working with many people over the years lead me to believe that there is a pattern with many of the people I've counselled.

Into every life a little rain must fall – we know that we will all experience life events but some people are affected more deeply by life events and find it much harder to cope with them and are therefore more prone to experiencing exogenous depression. In addition, it seems they are also more likely to suffer from endogenous depression – where there is no *obvious* external cause. This susceptibility appears to come from the fact that some people become 'threat sensitive' from quite early on in life. Threat sensitivity means that their filter is set to notice the potential negative facets of life from quite an early age.

The pattern seems to be that one of three possible factors is present in such people. One factor is that the threat sensitivity emanates from either the effects of nature or nurture (or both). Children can be influenced by threat sensitive parents (or other significant people) who view the world as a dangerous place and reinforce this view in their offspring. Some parents are repeatedly heard telling their children to be careful or warning them of the dangers of doing certain things. A second factor, which can happen to people either as children or young adults, is where something very traumatic happens to them in the form of some type of serious mental, physical or sexual abuse. The third factor is where a child or young person is brought up in circumstances whereby they experience generalised anxiety over a period of time. Examples of this may include where their parents divorce or if the family has difficult financial circumstances.

Let's look at the effects of nature and nurture first. Some children are born in circumstances where either one or both parents seem to be 'worriers'. These children are then brought up throughout their childhood and teenage years in an environment where mum or dad are frequently heard saying: "When you go out make sure you don't….." "Be careful you always remember to………….." "I really wouldn't do that, it could be very dangerous to…….." The **value** that gets reinforced is that it's a scary world full of potentially nasty, threatening people and situations that you should treat very carefully. So, either through the effects of nature or nurture the child becomes very threat sensitive which, in turn can lead to risk aversion. Daisy's parents were a classic example of the effects of nature/nurture.

When her company referred Daisy to me she had been off sick with stress for some time because her boss, the Sales Director, had been putting too much pressure on her and her colleagues in the sales team. Although the company had suspended the Sales Director for his actions they were very worried they would lose Daisy who was their top sales person. The company's HR Manager was mystified as to why Daisy, of all the sales team, had succumbed to stress. Daisy was easily the company's most successful sales person and had been for a few years. She was well liked by her colleagues and had a reputation for being easy to work with and was very conscientious in her dealings with both clients and the sales support staff at head office. The HR Manager described Daisy as almost the perfect employee and told me that Daisy would be a far greater loss to the company than the Sales Director. Despite all this, Daisy suffered from a chronic lack of confidence. The pressure she had been put under by the Sales Director had caused a raft of physiological and psychological symptoms resulting in a period of several weeks off sick with stress.

Where did Daisy's self-doubt come from? When I started working with Daisy she told me that she was the only child of older parents. Throughout her childhood, teenage and early adult life Daisy's parents worried about everything she did. Although Daisy was now in her early 30s and was very successful they still worried about Daisy's life choices and their worrying instilled a high degree of self-doubt in Daisy.

When Daisy first left school she decided to train to become a teacher. Her parents were very worried that she wouldn't be able to cope with classroom discipline because they were concerned about how unruly school children can be. Consequently they tried to dissuade Daisy from a teaching career and she spent weeks worrying before she plucked up the courage to take up her place at college.

Daisy managed to get a job in a school where the children were well behaved and she spent several quite successful years at the school. However, her Head Teacher, who wanted Daisy to take on extra responsibility put her under a lot of pressure. Daisy felt that she was being bullied. She spoke to her parents about the pressure from the Head Teacher and told them she wanted to leave the teaching profession. Her parents were very worried that she shouldn't leave the security of the teaching profession. Daisy tried to put up with the pressure because of her parents concerns about leaving the profession. However, eventually when the bullying became too much, Daisy found the courage to go against her parents' wishes and leave teaching.

Daisy then gained her Masters degree and decided she wanted to follow a career in business. Once again Daisy's parents expressed their doubts about the suitability of this course of action. The cut and thrust world of business was, in her parents' view, something to be very wary of. Daisy again agonised about whether she should follow her inclination before eventually finding a career in sales.

At the time I was working with Daisy she, and her long time partner, were thinking about starting a family at some point in the near future. Not surprisingly, Daisy's mum had already sewn the seeds of doubt in Daisy's mind about whether she would be able to handle the stress of parenthood and a career.

Throughout her life the influence of her parents had reinforced certain values about the type of world it was that Daisy lived in – difficult and dangerous. Whilst this had not prevented Daisy from following her career path, there was a cost she had to pay. The self-doubt instilled at an early age and reinforced throughout her teenage and early adult life resulted in several problems for Daisy. She was very easily intimidated by authority figures such as her Head Teacher and the Sales Director. She was inclined to agonise for long periods of time over decisions, particularly when her feelings were in conflict with her parents. The internal conflict had resulted in several periods of sickness from work with stress. Whilst daisy found the courage to ultimately face up to her self doubt there were times when it blighted her life.

The second factor relates to where a child or young adult experiences some form of traumatic mental, physical or sexual abuse. Once again, in these circumstances the **value** of not trusting people and looking out for the potential threats in a dangerous world is reinforced. Cathy's sad childhood years paint a clear picture of how this can happen.

Cathy was 7 years old when her parents split up. Without any apparent warning Cathy's mum left the family home to live with another man. Cathy's dad found it very difficult to cope with Cathy, and her younger brother John, and they were often left to their own devices whilst their dad went out. After a few years her dad found a new partner who didn't want anything to do with Cathy and John. So, their father decided that they would be better off being brought up by their aunt and uncle. Cathy's aunt was a lovely woman with no children of her own and she treated Cathy and John as her own children. Cathy's uncle began to sexually abuse Cathy when she was 12 years old.

Cathy's story is one of continually being let down by people, people that she should have been able to trust. Rejected by her mother, rejected by her father and then abused by her uncle, it's not difficult to see why Cathy continues to this day to view the world as a very dangerous place where no one can be trusted.

So, both frequently reinforced negative messages, and traumatic incidents can cause the filter to be set to notice the negative things in life. If an individual is exposed to either (or even worse, both) they are more prone to psychological distress later in life.
It's easy to see how Daisy and Cathy came to view the world in a particular way. Both of them were acutely aware of why they worried about things in life.

But sometimes it's not as clear to people why they have an unidentified generalised anxiety about life. I mentioned Lena earlier in the book. She had a good job, two lovely children, a caring husband and a beautiful house. There was nothing obvious about her depression, no clear external cause that she could pinpoint. Her depression was endogenous. She described it as a "little black spot on the sun." The more she talked about her childhood the clearer the explanation for her depression seemed to be. Her father, whilst he loved his family, had been a very strict disciplinarian who was prone to outbursts of temper when he was annoyed. Lena was very conscious of trying not to upset him by saying or doing the wrong thing.

Her father was a very clever man, who valued education but Lena dreaded him helping with her homework. When she was unable to understand his explanations he would lose his patience and curse her stupidity. Lena is a bright woman, but at school she was not particularly gifted in academic subjects. She wanted to be a hairdresser much to the disappointment of her father who was scathing about her choice of career.

I asked her how happy her childhood was. She pondered the question for a while and then said that she couldn't ever remember being really happy in her childhood. She thought for a while longer and then said that she realised she must have had lots of happy times as a child but she simply couldn't remember them. The overriding DVD memories were of being anxious about upsetting her father. Lena's filter had been subconsciously set to notice the potential pitfalls of upsetting her father and the negative consequences if she did. It's a habit that she hadn't been able to break and had left her with a susceptibility to endogenous depression. However, it wasn't until she started counselling that Lena consciously recognised the negative effect of her relationship with her father.

People who are prone to psychological distress become threat sensitive. Their filters have been set to notice the unpleasant, dangerous things in life, and the DVD memories that make it through the filter tend to be of negative past experiences or future potential negative outcomes. Consequently they also become quite risk averse and less likely to take chances or seize opportunities. Both threat sensitivity and risk aversion are features of people who tend towards the **trait** of pessimism and this is likely to be reflected in certain **styles**.

The dangers of pessimism.
It seems that some people, like Lena, Daisy and Cathy, are more prone to pessimism than others. The negative effects of pessimism have been well documented in recent years. The writers Donald Clifton and Tom Rath (1) have produced some excellent work linking pessimism to earlier death rates, poorer health and less success in life. Martin Seligman, in his research on optimism and pessimism, notes that at work, school and in sport, optimists stay with difficult and challenging situations whilst pessimists don't do so well and often give up. Seligman and Schulman's (2) classic experiment with life

insurance sales people showed this quite clearly. They studied life insurance sales people, an industry where sales people experience frequent rejection and have a high drop out rate. Seligman and Schulman found that the sales people who were the most optimistic significantly out performed those who were pessimistic.

Of course, not everyone who was brought up in an environment of anxiety or fear goes on to be threat sensitive. Not everyone who had parents who were themselves prone to worrying turns out to be pessimistic. Not everyone who experiences a trauma when they are relatively young goes on to be susceptible to depression in later years. However, if you were unfortunate enough to have had your filter set to notice the negative DVD memories in life when you were relatively young then you will be more **likely** to have a predisposition towards suffering stress, anxiety and depression. Since our values, traits and styles are relatively fixed and enduring once we reach a certain age this reinforces the idea of certain people having a predisposition towards being less emotionally resilient.

However, there are plenty of emotionally resilient people who suffer a very negative experience or life event later on in life, which temporarily causes their filter to be re-set from noticing the positives to noticing the negatives. The people I've counselled over the years fall into both camps. Those with a predisposition towards pessimism and those who would normally class themselves as optimists but whose emotional resilience has been overwhelmed by a series of life events.

The myth of weak characters.
People succumb to the effects of psychological distress because of the way their values, traits and style interact with the prevailing external situation they find themselves in. Depression, anxiety and stress are due in part to the sufferers' predisposition towards threat sensitivity and in part to the particular circumstances they find themselves in.

It's important not to think of people who struggle with life events as being somehow 'weak characters' and those who seem to cope well as being 'strong characters'. However, many people fall into this trap. This is one of the reasons why people who suffer from aspects of psychological distress get less sympathy than someone suffering from an obvious tangible physical ailment. The tendency is to assume that it is the depressed person's inherent inability to cope with their life that is the main reason for their depressed state. Whilst this certainly plays a part, we should not underestimate the difficulty of the circumstances they may currently find themselves exposed to.

Psychologists call this tendency to attribute the outcome in a situation to the person's response to the situation rather than the situation itself, Fundamental Attribution Error (FAE). The term comes from the research on attribution (3). In the context of depression it simply means that we have a tendency to attribute the depressed state to the individual's traits rather than attributing it to their circumstances. Most people placed in certain very stressful situations will react in a similar way. This was demonstrated in a famous experiment conducted by psychologist Stanley Milgram (4) in the 1960s. He asked a group of volunteers to take part in what they thought was a learning experiment conducted by a very authoritarian figure. The man in charge of the experiment told each volunteer that a subject in the next room was trying to complete a task. The volunteer was asked to observe the subject and each time the subject made a mistake the volunteer was told to administer an electric shock to the subject. In reality the subject was an actor and the equipment for giving the electric shocks was a dummy piece of equipment.

During the experiment the man in charge was able to get the volunteer to increase the voltage of the shock by telling the volunteer how important it was for the purpose of the experiment that they continued to keep administering shocks to the subject. Despite the subject's increasingly distressed responses to the 'pain' of the shocks about two thirds of the volunteers continued to increase the voltage under the pressure from the man in charge of the experiment. Some volunteers were even persuaded to give shocks when the 'dial' on the equipment reached a red section that said 450 volts.

When they hear about this experiment most people don't believe that they would give the subject the electric shocks. However, this experiment has been replicated many times with very consistent results – about two thirds of the volunteers for this type of experiment can be persuaded to give another person an electric shock under the right conditions. The reason for this is as much to do with the circumstances as it is to do with the individual volunteers.

By the same token, most people will probably experience psychological distress when they are faced with emotional life events. Unfortunately, if we place too much emphasis on a person's traits it encourages people who succumb to the stress of the life event to believe they are 'weak characters'. In turn this makes it very difficult to admit to suffering from stress because of the stigma that is sometimes associated with it. FAE may also account for the lack of sympathy for sufferers of depression, stress and anxiety, particularly from friends or colleagues who are themselves very emotionally resilient. I have occasionally heard Human Resource professionals being somewhat surprised that an individual has been signed off sick from work because of the stress of what HR people deem relatively minor stressful circumstances.

The Roman Emperor, Marcus Aurelius, whose life was mainly spent trying to hold back the barbarians from the Roman frontier, eloquently sums up this concept. "Tell yourself each morning: today I shall meet an envious chap, an ungrateful one and a bully, and if I had their life I could easily become one too." So, to sum up, some people are more prone to depression than others because of certain experiences in their lives, which make them more pessimistic. However, we all have the capacity to be depressed if certain external factors are present in our lives. Furthermore, if these factors are present early enough in our lives they make a very big impression in the formation of our values, traits and styles.

This is well illustrated by my own father's experience as a child. My Dad, Paul, is a truly wonderful man who has had a very interesting life. He was born in India, the son of an English mother and a Greek father who was a senior administrator on the vast Indian railway network. Almost as soon as he was born his parents decided that because they spent a lot of their life travelling around the Indian sub continent it would be better if Paul was brought up by his grandparents and his unmarried Aunt Ellene. So my dad spent his childhood and teenage years in his grandparents house being looked after to a great degree by his Aunt Ellene. His sense of rejection by his own parents must have been heightened when at the age of two his parents had another son, his brother Peter, who, for some reason his parents decided to keep with them.

I remember my dad telling me that most evenings after he was put to bed by Ellene she would leave his grandparents to baby-sit whilst she cycled off to the club to socialise. Whenever this happened my Dad would get up, sit by his bedroom window and wait. Only when he saw the lights on her bicycle lamp as she returned from the club would he be able to settle down to sleep. It's easy to imagine that little boy's sense of worry and concern as he looked out of his window into the Indian night – he had already been rejected by his mother and father, and the thought of his surrogate mother not returning must have played on his mind considerably.

As I write this book my dad is now in his 80s. Throughout his life he has had a tendency to worry about many things and has been, by his own description, a pessimist.

Despite this, he was a successful officer during WWII reaching the rank of Major at only 21. He later graduated from Cambridge University and had a wonderful career as a teacher and a college lecturer as well as writing several books. In addition he has also been a wonderful father and grandfather. He has managed his pessimism quite well over the years and has been helped in this by a deep Catholic faith and a wife, my mother, who was very optimistic. After my Mum died a few years ago, quite understandably he has slipped back towards his natural pessimism.

Much of my work involves travelling around the country and I often stay at my Dad's house overnight if I am working in that region of the country. If I am even a few minutes later than my estimated time of arrival at his house he calls me on my mobile phone to check everything is okay. The little boy is still looking out of the window.

It bothers my Dad that he is like this. He sees it as a personal failing that he worries so much and does not have more faith that things will turn out okay. The worry has made him inclined not to take risks and he feels he has missed out on some excellent opportunities because he always took the safe route in his career. Whilst he had a very successful career in education, his great yearning in life was to be a barrister but he did not have the confidence to pursue this riskier career. He is highly critical of himself and he rarely stops to wonder why he worries so much. He is making a Fundamental Attribution Error – most people, if they had experienced his childhood would have a tendency to worry about the future.

A balanced view – changing perceptions.

We are who we are - know thyself. My role as a psychologist is not to try to change people, it's to help people better understand themselves and the situations they find themselves in. If people understand how the interplay between their internal world (values, traits and styles) and their external world (life events) can lead to a depressed mood state they can begin to move forward. From this perspective they are able to reflect on why they are making the thinking errors which hold the filter in place so that predominantly negative DVD memories are filtered into their conscious mind. It's not about changing people, it's about helping people to change their perception of life. In essence my job is to help my clients to have a more positive perception of themselves and their situation. Later on in the book we will look at how to start the process of getting a balanced view of life by beginning the process of perceptual change.

Summary of Chapter 5. Self-knowledge.

Susceptibility to psychological distress. It seems that some people may be more likely to suffer from psychological distress than others. In particular this appears to be true of endogenous depression. The trigger for this susceptibility seems to emanate from one of three sources. Firstly, the inheritance of pessimistic values/traits from their parents, secondly as a result of being subjected to some form of abuse. Thirdly, through a generalised anxiety about the environment they are brought up in. The consequence of any of these factors is a susceptibility to being both threat sensitive and risk averse which are characteristics of pessimism.

The dangers of pessimism. Pessimism seems to be linked to poorer health, lower life expectancy, lower levels of success and it's just less fun than being optimistic. Worse than this, it can also lead to the self-fulfilling prophecies mentioned earlier in the book. If we believe that things will go wrong we increase the likelihood that they will.

The myth of weak characters. Some people seem to cope better with life events than others. However, this does not make some people 'strong' characters and others 'weak' characters. It seems that generally we have a desire to want to explain a person's success or failure in coping with a particular situation by attributing it to the individual rather than accepting that the situation itself may have had a big part in deciding the outcome. Fundamental Attribution Error (FAE) is the name given to this phenomenon. Most people placed in difficult, challenging situations would probably respond in a broadly similar fashion – they would all experience a degree of stress.

A balanced view – changing perceptions. Helping people with psychological distress is about providing them with the tools to change their perception of themselves and their lives, the interplay between their internal and external worlds. It's not about fundamentally changing them as individuals. We are who we are. To understand ourselves better makes us more accepting of our internal world and our ability to relate to the external world.

CHAPTER 6.
CONTROL AND LETTING GO.

I was once teaching a post graduate class for American teachers in Ohio USA. As the first session of the class unfolded, one woman who seemed to have quite a forceful, dominant character intrigued me. In the discussions we were having about what made an effective learning environment this woman's views were quite clear on the role that the teacher should play. She seemed a little dismissive of the views of other people in the class who felt that the students should play a part in deciding their own environment. As the temperature rose later in the day, this lady removed her sweatshirt and underneath she wore a tee shirt with the simple message "Because I'm the teacher!" Believing we can control other people's behaviour because of our position of authority can easily set us up for failure. The only person's behaviour we can truly control is our own.

The issue of control is closely linked to the concept of changing our perceptions in order to get a more balanced perspective on our lives, which we discussed in the last chapter. Broadly speaking, the more control we feel we have, then the more positive DVD memories we will store in the library in our mind and the better the balance between positive and negative DVD memories. If we focus on controlling our own behaviour in order to try to influence other people to make positive choices we will experience more success than if we believe we can control other people's behaviour through sheer force of personality.

The concept of control.
Many of the depressed people I've worked with over the years feel quite unable to control their lives. This lack of control is closely linked to the curse of self-doubt, the lack of confidence and the loss of self-esteem we talked about in chapters 2 and 3. As I mentioned earlier when we experience psychological distress it's because there is a poor fit between our internal world (values, traits and styles) and our external world (life events). The perceived lack of control that

emanates from this poor fit can be a contributory cause to a depressed mood state.

Research on British civil servants (1) suggested that the more control they felt they had over their work then the lower the levels of stress they experienced. Whilst this seems a pretty logical conclusion the relationship between control and stress may be slightly more complex. There doesn't appear to be any argument over the idea that the more control we have over our lives the less stressed we feel. However, in my experience it seems apparent that some people who have relatively little or even no control over a situation experience relatively low levels of distress - providing they can 'let it go'.

The highest levels of stress seem to occur when someone can neither control a situation fully nor let it go. Accepting that we have relatively little control over certain factors in a situation can be very liberating – providing that we then channel our energies into the factors that we can control. The following graph shows how this works.

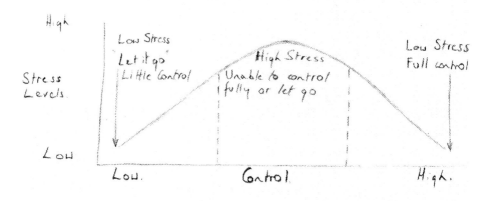

Eleanor came to me in a very depressed state. Her marriage was in difficulty, the family was experiencing financial hardship and she was struggling to cope with her job. In addition, the biggest difficulty she faced was that her two sons aged 9 and 11 were constantly challenging her parenting skills. She was visibly upset as she described taking her sons to school one day. On arriving outside the school gates both sons refused to get out of the car. The eldest one eventually decided to get out and go into the school playground. However the youngest son, Phillip, simply refused to leave the car. In desperation, she opened the front passenger door to try to take hold of his arm in order to physically march him into the school playground. As she approached the passenger door Phillip jumped across to the drivers seat and hid down by the pedals where his mum couldn't reach him. As Eleanor ran round to the driver's door Phillip jumped back to the other seat and hid on the floor where again she could not reach him. This game of cat and mouse continued for several minutes with Eleanor becoming more and more stressed much to the bemusement of other parents dropping their children off. Eventually she managed to catch hold of Phillip's arm and literally dragged him out of the car. As Eleanor frog-marched him across the playground Phillip threw himself down on the floor and began to shout and scream drawing the attention of the other children and parents to Eleanor's predicament. Eleanor's humiliation was complete when one of the teachers came out and told Phillip to get up immediately, stop shouting and go into school, a request he complied with straight away.

As Eleanor recounted this story the tears rolled down her face. She felt a complete failure as a parent when her inability to control her son's behaviour was played out in a very public arena under the gaze of parents and teachers some of whom expressed quite judgmental views about Eleanor's parenting skills.

"Whose behaviour can you control completely?" I asked her. She paused for a long time before replying "Only my own." It's quite a difficult realisation for many parents to accept that their children have a mind of their own, which won't necessarily be influenced by their parents' wishes.

Choices and Consequences.
We talked for a while about how she could try to influence her son to behave in a more appropriate way through using the concept of 'choices and consequences' which we touched upon earlier in

this book. William Glasser (2) uses the philosophy of choices and consequences in much of his work.

Listening to Eleanor it became clear that she was frequently engaged in arguments with both her sons. She had become very 'threat sensitive'. Every time Eleanor got up in the morning she was sub-consciously looking for every little thing that was negative about the children's behaviour. She constantly challenged them about their behaviour, which had the effect of provoking the rows.

Eleanor recognised that the negative things about the children were much more noticeable because she was dealing with some very difficult life events relating to her marriage, job and finances. The threat sensitivity, which emanated from the life events, was seriously impacting her relationship with the children. This led Eleanor to feel doubt about her ability as a parent, in turn her confidence and self esteem were decreasing and this was resulting in a self fulfilling prophecy as she found herself increasingly less able to deal effectively with Phillip's behaviour.

Our plan to help Eleanor was fairly simple. Firstly Eleanor had to accept that she couldn't control the childrens' behaviour, she could only control her own behaviour. This meant that despite the childrens' outbursts Eleanor would control her own temper and not rise to the bait. Secondly, I asked Eleanor to work out which two or three aspects of the childrens' behaviour were completely unacceptable. One of these aspects was, not surprisingly, the refusal to go to school. These were to be our 'hills worth dying for', the rest of their behaviour we deemed 'background noise' which was not worth getting into an argument over.

Next, Eleanor would make it absolutely clear to the children that if they chose to ignore Eleanor on the 'hill' issues there would be negative consequences. If they chose to work with her on the hill issues there would be positive consequences. If Eleanor recognised that the children were making 'background noise' she would just ignore the behaviour.

When we first discussed it Eleanor seemed a little uneasy that she should simply ignore some of the childrens' behaviour. So I asked her how effective, in terms of changing their behaviour, was her current strategy of challenging them on every issue. She paused for a while before she smiled ruefully and admitted that it hadn't succeeded. I pointed out to her that it was quite possible that our plan to change their behaviour wouldn't work either, but at least by controlling her own behaviour she wouldn't have the stress and anxiety of the rows.

Eventually she began to realise that it was okay to accept that she couldn't control the behaviour of her 9 and 11 year-old children completely. However, as long as she controlled her own behaviour she felt calmer and more in control of the situation. This in turn allowed her to use the strategy of explaining to the children that it was their decision about whether to chose to behave in an unacceptable way but that their choice would involve certain consequences with regard to future treats.

This example demonstrates beautifully how accepting that we can't control some things allows us to put more energy into affecting what we can control. Eleanor accepted she could not directly control Phillip's behaviour, but by remaining calm and not playing the games that Phillip wanted to engage her in she felt calmer and therefore more able to deal with the situation.

Accepting our limitations and channelling our energies into what we can control makes us feel better. In turn, this allows us to accept our limitations more easily. Because we are focusing on the positive DVD memories of what we are able to control we have less self-doubt, and our self-esteem and confidence benefit which helps lead to a more positive self-fulfilling prophecy.

The next time Phillip began to play the game of refusing to get out of the car Eleanor's strategy worked very effectively. She had previously explained her problem to Phillip's teacher and warned the teacher that although Phillip might be late for school she wanted the teacher's support to address this problem. The teacher was happy to provide this support when she understood Eleanor's dilemma. Eleanor also pre-warned her boss that she might be a little bit late to work because she was having difficulties with her son but she would happily make the time up. Once again she got a positive response from her boss. This made Eleanor feel more in control and confident before she even arrived at school.

When Phillip began his game of jumping from seat to seat. Eleanor got back into the driver's seat and told Phillip calmly that it was his choice whether he continued to play this game but that she was not prepared to play it with him. She went on to explain why she wanted him to get out of the car and walk into school like the other children and that if he chose not to do this he would not be allowed to play with his friends after school. Phillip initially refused to leave the car and Eleanor said that she thought it was a shame but if he chose not to comply with her request that was his choice, the consequence was that he would not be able to play with his friends. Phillip began to shout and scream that it was unfair. Eleanor calmly picked up her newspaper and started reading it. Eventually Phillip calmed down and when he did Eleanor asked him very politely if he would please get out of the car and walk with her into school. After a few minutes Phillip left the car quietly and Eleanor thanked him as they walked together into school. She also promised him that if he were good about getting out of the car tomorrow he would be able to play with his friends after school.

Eleanor was able to control her own responses to Phillip's behaviour. She was also able to successfully influence Phillip's teacher and her own boss to support her in dealing with Phillip's behaviour. This increased her feelings of control over the situation. Regardless of how Phillip behaved she would have a positive DVD memory stored of how she successfully controlled her own behaviour and got support from two key people. There are two further potential benefits that can result from this. Firstly, if Eleanor has a difficult day in the future and she loses her patience with Phillip (which will almost certainly happen because she's only human!) she will be able to counter the thinking error that "I never seem to be able to deal calmly with Phillip". She can search her mental DVD library and she will find the positive DVD of her dealing calmly with his temper outburst which will disprove the thinking error that she can't deal calmly with him. Secondly, she will be better able to break the cycle of pessimistic self-fulfilling prophecy. The confidence she has gained from dealing with Phillip calmly in the past will increase her belief that she can do it successfully again in the future.

Getting a balanced perspective on control.
In life a balanced perspective is important and finding equilibrium is vital for good psychological health. An understanding of what we can control and what we have very little control over is an example of equilibrium. I work quite closely with a very successful senior executive at a technology company - Andrew. One of the reasons that Andrew is so successful is that he has a very strong belief that he can personally control the outcome of his work in a favourable way. Andrew has a very strong internal attribution – he attributes his success or failure in any situation to what he personally does or doesn't do. He tries to instil this in all the people who work for him. "I get very frustrated when people tell me it's never their fault. Either the project manager is to blame for the customer's dissatisfaction, it's the sales team fault the deal went wrong, or their cat was ill this morning so they couldn't get here on time - everyone else was to blame except them".

However, when I dig a little deeper with Andrew he does understand that sometimes the situation itself makes it much more difficult to control the final outcome. His frustration is with people who haven't worked out what they can control and consequently haven't channelled their energies into this aspect of their work. He also gets frustrated with people who are either not honest about their weaknesses, or who simply don't know themselves well enough to realise they have certain weaknesses. This is another element of knowing what you can and can't control. Andrew manages to balance FAE quite finely – he wants people to channel their energies into trying to control the factors that can be controlled. He doesn't have a problem if they don't have the necessary strengths to do it themselves so long as they recognise this and ask for help where they need it.

For example, Andrew was responsible for managing a very bright young man - Nicholas. Nick was working on a deal with a large telecoms company who wanted to buy an IT system from Andrew's company. Nick had overall responsibility for the deal and Andrew was very worried about the amount of money that was being spent in order to win the deal – the 'pre-sales costs'. Nick was responsible for pre-sales costs but a salesman, Joe, who did not work directly for Nick was incurring much of the cost. The situation itself was difficult – Nick was responsible for the costs but the person incurring the costs, Joe, was not line managed directly by Nick. Andrew sat down with Nick several times and re-iterated the importance of keeping the pre-sales costs down. He suggested ways for Nick to help Joe understand the problem, and went on to describe how Nick could conduct a meeting with Joe to get the outcome Nick needed. However, Nick was at pains to point out to Andrew how single-minded and assertive Joe was in wanting to win this deal whatever the cost.

After several discussions there seemed to be no discernible improvement in the pre-sales costs. So Andrew asked me to have a chat with Nick to see if I could help coach him through this situation. I also conducted a number of psychometric tests with Nick to try to identify the traits where he was naturally strong and the areas where he was less effective. The tests seemed to show that Nick had many talents. However, dealing with very dominant assertive individuals did not appear to be one of them and hence it was easy to see why Nick found this element of his role difficult. I gently tried to help Nick to interpret the results so that he would be able to recognise that perhaps the situation wasn't playing to his strengths. Unfortunately Nick was categoric that he was very adept at dealing with assertive people successfully, despite the contrary evidence of both the tests and the real life data of the escalating pre-sales costs.

"What Andrew doesn't understand is that Joe has spent 18 months trying to win this deal, he's put his heart and soul into it and he's so close to winning the deal he just won't listen to anyone". Nick's rationale was that it was solely the situation that was driving the outcome of increasing pre-sales costs. However, in the process of doing this he was admitting he had no control over the situation, which was very dis-empowering for him. It would have been far better for Nick to admit that he wasn't particularly effective at dealing assertively with the salesman. Had he done this we could have looked at alternative strategies to try to change the situation so that it played to Nick's strengths. I noticed that Nick was very strong in areas that involved analysing data and drawing conclusions. I suggested that Nick might want to approach Maria, Joe's boss, with a very reasoned analysis of the escalating costs of pre-sales. I was certain that Andrew, who had a good relationship with Maria, would assist in the process of getting Nick a meeting with Maria. However, to meet with Maria meant admitting his own failures in not being able to assert his views on Joe. Nick opted not to heed the advice and eventually Andrew moved Nick to another part of the business more suited to his skills and replaced him with someone who was able to control the pre-sales costs incurred by Joe.

This example demonstrates the fine balance needed with control. The problem lay partly in the difficulty of the situation and partly in Nick's inability to deal with the situation. It was about the interplay between Nick's internal world (values, traits and styles) and the external situation of a headstrong salesman determined to win a deal whatever the cost. As I mentioned in the Human Factors model, our mood is determined by how close the fit is between our internal and external worlds - pegs and holes. Nick couldn't change who he was, he couldn't suddenly become a very dominant, assertive individual who was going to impose his authority on the maverick salesman Joe. He had to accept that he couldn't control this. What he could do, if he was prepared to accept himself for who he was, was to try to control the situation in a different way. By approaching Maria and using his analytical strengths he could have got her to impose her authority on the salesman, but his unwillingness to accept himself got in the way.

So, accept what we can't control and channel our energies into what we can control - balance.

Getting a balanced perspective on optimism.
In taking our theme of balance further it's important to look at the concept of optimism again. In the earlier discussion on the brain's filter, the RAS, we noted that when our filter has been set to notice all the negative things in our lives that we lose a balanced perspective. The more we play the negative DVD memories, the greater our self-doubt and the less we feel able to control or influence many aspects of our lives. In turn, this can lead to pessimism and negative self-fulfilling prophecy.

However, whilst it's an advantage to be broadly optimistic about life, blind optimism can be quite damaging too; it's not a balanced view of life. Earlier when I drew the model of the filter with black and white DVDs I pointed out the dangers of having our filters set to allow only the black negative DVDs through the filter. It's important to recognise, though, that only allowing the white DVDs through the filter also shows a lack of perspective and balance.

Jim Collins in his book, 'Good to Great' (3) talks about the Stockdale Paradox, which recognises the importance of acknowledging the brutal truth of a negative situation whilst, at the same time, being broadly optimistic that the situation will improve. The Stockdale Paradox is named after Admiral Stockdale, the highest-ranking officer in the US Navy who was captured by the North Vietnamese during the Vietnam War.

Stockdale noticed that when first captured some servicemen were unrealistically optimistic about how soon the war would be over and when they would be repatriated. The psychological well being of these individuals deteriorated most rapidly when time passed and they were still imprisoned. Their initial confidence that "we'll all be home by Christmas" was severely dented when Christmas had come and gone and they were still imprisoned. The servicemen who fared best during their imprisonment were those who faced the brutal truth

– that they wouldn't be home by Christmas – but who also never stopped believing that they would eventually be repatriated with their families.

People in captivity offer an interesting perspective on how they combine a balanced perspective on both optimism and control. In most respects prisoners have very little control over their lives because their freedom has been taken from them. The story of Victor Frankel (4) offers a wonderfully uplifting insight into this concept. Frankel was an Austrian Jew who was imprisoned by the Nazis in the brutally dehumanising concentration camp of Auschwitz. The concentration camp's daily routine consisted of unimaginable physical and mental tortures. Prisoners were slowly starved to death with only rags to keep them warm and the constant threat of the gas chambers. Frankel had already seen several members of his family taken to the gas chambers and murdered. It would have been very understandable if he had completely given up hope as so many of his fellow prisoners did. Frankel had been a University Professor before his imprisonment and as he endured his incarceration he tried to visualise himself in the future lecturing to a large group of students about his experiences in Auschwitz. He imagined what he would like to be able to tell them he had learned about human nature from his experiences. He realised that if, in the future, he wanted to be able to tell a positive story about his experiences then he had to live out those positive experiences in the here and now. So he set about creating a series of positive DVD memories that he could use in the future. The only thing he could control was his own attitude and behaviour so he became as supportive as he possibly could to his fellow prisoners, talking to them, sympathising with them, showing them every kindness he could. He became a wonderful source of inspiration, not only for the other prisoners but also for some of the guards. Like Stockdale, he was planning for the day when he got released. Frankel was balancing the brutal truth with an optimism born of trying to control as much of his life as possible by creating positive DVD memories in his present situation that he could then use in his student lectures in the future.

Frankel said "Everything can be taken away from us but one thing, the last human freedom, to choose one's own attitude in any given set of circumstances to choose our own way."

These examples help to demonstrate the importance of balance. If we are able to get a balanced perspective we can even appreciate the poignancy of very difficult emotional situations and become stronger as a result. We are also able to accept ourselves in a much less judgmental way, which decreases our self-doubt and increases our self-esteem.

Summary of Chapter 6. Control and letting go.

The concept of control. Traditional thought suggests that the more control we have over a situation the less stress or anxiety we experience. This may be a view that is over simplified. It is possible to have low levels of control *and* low levels of stress if we can accept that there are some things we can't control and we channel our energies into controlling the factors that can be controlled. Focussing on what we can control can lead to positive DVDs being played and an increase in our self-confidence. Understanding that some factors in a situation can't be controlled avoids the self-doubt that creeps in when we view ourselves in the context of thinking errors. This is summed up by the thinking error on Personalisation, 'seeing yourself or someone else as the cause of some negative external event which the individual was not responsible for'.

Choices and Consequences. Accepting that other people have choices about how they behave and that all we can do is try to influence their choices through controlling our own behaviour can be quite liberating. Helping others to understand that there are potential positive and negative consequences for their behaviour helps them to make better choices.

Getting a balanced perspective on control. Making every effort to control what we genuinely can leads to internalising our attribution and can empower us. However, it's important to get the balance right: beating ourselves up over things we can't control increases our sense of failure but making excuses and blaming other people when we could have influenced a situation dis-empowers us.

Getting a balanced perspective on pessimism. Whilst the dangers of pessimism are well documented, blind optimism can be almost as dangerous. The Stockdale Paradox sums this up neatly: face up to the brutal truth in a situation, don't delude yourself whilst at the same time remain broadly optimistic that if you focus on what you can control, the situation will eventually turn out positively.

CHAPTER 7.
SHOCK AND AWE.

So far this book has tried to provide an explanation of what happens in the mind of someone who is suffering from some form of psychological distress. We have looked at the links between thinking errors and the filter causing negative DVD memories to predominate in the form of negative introspection, which subsequently leads to self-doubt, lack of confidence, low self-esteem and negative self-fulfilling prophecy. This chapter will look at why our mind goes through this process and in particular, how it reacts to very traumatic life events in order to try to protect us in the short term.

The mind's immune system.
As I've mentioned before our mind is a very complex and powerful piece of equipment. Whenever we are emotionally troubled our mind automatically tries to help us get through our difficulties. In a similar way to our physiological immune system, our mind works to help protect us against our emotional troubles. However, it seems that the mind's immune system is programmed for short-term protection rather than long term solutions. When we experience emotionally difficult times our conscious mind is alerted to look out for potentially threatening situations because of it's sensitivity to negative DVD memories from the past which have been allowed through the filter from the sub-conscious mind.

In the case of Lena, who I mentioned earlier, this was how her mind worked. Her father was a very intimidating man who was quick to lose his patience when annoyed. When Lena's father returned home after work Lena's mind had already been programmed to watch out for danger signals, such as whether he was in a bad mood, her mind was preparing her for the worst so she could take appropriate action. Unfortunately for Lena, her filter had been set so effectively to enable her conscious mind to actively look for the danger signals from her father's behaviour that it generalised this pattern of thinking. The thinking errors extended to look for all the negative things in her life and so the filter was set. This thought pattern continued for many years after she left home and no longer needed to be aware of the potential threats from her father's irritable temper. The immune system strategy may have worked in the short term, but not in the long term.

Another aspect of the sub-conscious mind trying to help us through our emotional difficulties occurs when we are faced with traumatic life events. Sometimes, the only way we feel we can deal with a very painful event is *not* to deal with it. When we are in shock over something incredibly painful our mind operates in a radically different way to help us cope. The immune system detects the DVD memory responsible for the pain and isolates it in a part of the mind's DVD library, in effect it puts the memory into quarantine. The DVD is then placed in a box and a heavy weight is put on the lid of the box to prevent it from springing open.

Perhaps the best example of this I've come across is the story of Louise who I mentioned earlier in the book. When I met Louise she was a successful designer in her late thirties. When she was much younger Louise had moved away from home to study Art at college and whilst she was studying she met Gary who was a very successful business executive quite a few years older than her. After a fairly short romance they decided to get married and moved into Gary's house in a neighbourhood where many of Gary's friends, family and work colleagues lived close by. For the first year of their marriage everything seemed fine. However, one night when they were in bed together Gary wanted to have sex but Louise felt too tired. Instead of accepting Louise's wishes, Gary raped her. In the few months that followed this first incident, Gary raped Louise several times, sometimes quite violently.

Louise was a young woman living hundreds of miles away from her home, married to an older, very successful, man; living in his house, with lots of his friends, colleagues and family close by. It's easy to question why she didn't leave Gary the first time it happened, but we would be guilty of FAE if we did that. Many women, like Louise, are abused physically, sexually and emotionally within what appears to be a stable relationship. Many women endure such abuse for years. It is the situation that these women find themselves in, rather than their own 'weakness' that results in them staying in the relationship. Fortunately for Louise she was eventually able to pluck up courage and leave Gary.

Keeping the lid on the box.
After Louise left she moved back home to her parents. She never told anyone about what happened to her. She didn't even acknowledge it to herself. She took those particularly painful DVD memories of the rapes and put them in a box on a high shelf in the DVD library in her mind. Louise then put a heavy weight on the box to make sure it didn't spring open. The DVD was in quarantine and Louise didn't want to let those incredibly powerful negative memories 'infect' the rest of her mind

If Louise never looked at those DVD memories she could pretend they didn't happen. The technique proved quite successful, at least up to a point. For the next 20 years she never once spoke about the rapes or acknowledged they happened. Then for some inexplicable reason, probably prompted by some unconscious trigger, she found herself blurting out her experiences to a particularly intuitive close friend. Once the DVD memories were out of the box she had great difficulty not playing them over in her mind. Not surprisingly, the more she played the DVDs, the more they 'infected' her mind and she became anxious, distressed and depressed in a fairly short period of time.

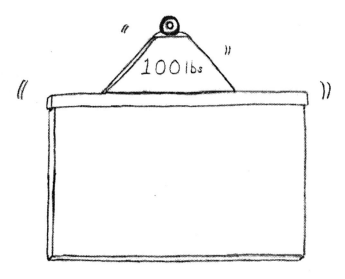

John Gray (1), in his excellent book on relationships, 'Venus and Mars starting over', points out the importance of properly acknowledging the negative emotions of fear, anger, sadness and sorrow. If we try to bury them, then we find it more difficult to experience the positive emotions in our lives. In effect this is what happened to Louise. She kept the lid on the box because she felt that if she opened the lid her mind would be infected and then overwhelmed by her negative emotions. She was worried that the fear, anger, sadness and sorrow would rush out of the box when the DVD memories were playing, engulf her mind and wreak havoc. However, the very act of keeping the lid on the box made it more difficult for Louise to experience positive emotions such as joy, happiness and hope.

As I mentioned earlier, the technique of quarantining the DVD memory in the box and securing it with a heavy weight was successful up to a point for Louise. However, there was a cost for her. John Gray's description of finding it hard to experience the positive emotions if you are burying the negative ones was an accurate description of what happened to Louise. Not surprisingly, she found it very hard to have relationships with men after what happened to her with Gary. For many years she simply didn't bother, fearful that any type of relationship with a man would trigger the box to spring open and play the painful DVD memories of the rapes.

Some years later when it seemed that Louise had perfected the trick of keeping the heavy weight balanced on the lid of the box, she started to engage in relationships with men. However, because she had buried the DVD memory and the subsequent negative emotions, she found it hard to experience the positive emotions of a close relationship. Perhaps even more damaging for the relationship she was unable to tell her partner why she was finding it difficult to get emotionally close. Having to explain herself would involve acknowledging the existence of the DVD memory and almost inevitably this would start the DVD playing.

Keeping the lid on the box is hard work. Ensuring the heavy weight stays in place to make certain the box doesn't fly open takes a lot of effort. All this effort reinforces the fact that there is a box of negative DVD memories in the library ready to infect the sufferer's mind if the lid flies open. The person's sub-conscious mind becomes acutely aware of this negative aspect of their life quarantined in the box. In turn this prompts the filter to keep searching for dangerous triggers that could cause the box to spring open. In Louise's case this involved self-sabotage. The closer she became with a partner the more likely she was to end the relationship. Alternatively, the more her partner got frustrated with Louise's reluctance to become emotionally close, the more likely he was to end the relationship. Louise now understands this, and she is actively working to come to terms with what happened to her.

Lifting the lid off the box.
It's only by deliberately and gradually releasing the lid of the box that we can start to come to terms with traumatic life events. In an ideal situation a good counsellor can help to do this. Even talking to close supportive friends, who won't judge, blame or offer well meaning, but perhaps inappropriate advice, can help to gradually open the box. To use the immune system analogy, releasing the lid off the box gradually is like allowing some anti-bodies into our mind so we can gradually build up our immunity.

Hilary, who I mentioned earlier, was someone who was able to release the lid on the box very gradually and successfully. Hilary came to see me about six months after her 19-year-old son Terry had committed suicide by taking an overdose. Hilary and her husband were professional people, she was a call centre manager and he was an accountant. They had three children in their teens and Terry was the middle child. Terry had always seemed to find life difficult. Hilary subsequently believed that Terry suffered from an undiagnosed learning difficulty at school and this may have been at the root of some of his problems.

Although Terry was a bright young man he had failed to get any qualifications from school and had left at 16. Terry moved in a circle of friends for whom drugs and crime were a way of life. Terry used drugs regularly and had been arrested by the police on several occasions. Hilary had worked hard to try to support Terry but she was unwilling to allow him to live in the family home because of the negative effect his way of life was having on his siblings. She managed to find Terry a flat and helped him to furnish it. Terry was a frequent visitor to the family home where he was always made welcome. He often shared meals with the family and remained quite close to them. He was, by all accounts, a cheerful roguish character with a certain charm. However, his drug habit made him unpredictable and often he would lose his temper and argue with the family, occasionally coming to blows with his father.

Hilary was very clear about how she tried to help Terry. She would support him emotionally, feed him if he came to the house and try to help him practically with looking after his flat. She never stopped loving him. However, she was determined that as long as he chose a life of petty crime and drugs she would not tolerate him living at home.

About a year before his death Terry began a relationship with Gemma. Hilary noticed a lot of positive changes in his behaviour. For the first time in his life he seemed to have more interest in getting and maintaining a job. The violent outbursts subsided. Terry decided to give up drugs and crime, and as a result of Gemma's influence he became a more stable person.

Unfortunately, after a few months he drifted back into drugs and crime and lost his job and although every few weeks he would try to make an effort to clean up his act, eventually Gemma decided to end the relationship.

Terry became quite depressed and Hilary increased her efforts to try to support him emotionally. Once again he decided to find work and give up his drug habit. Having successfully done this he took Gemma out for dinner one night in an attempt to persuade her to re-establish their relationship. Despite telling Terry that she really cared for him, Gemma didn't want to risk going back to the rollercoaster life style she had previously experienced with Terry.

Terry visited Hilary the next day to tell her of his disappointment. At the time Hilary thought he had taken it quite well, but within 36 hours his father found Terry dead in his flat having taken an overdose.

Hilary was devastated. She had been at work the night that her husband had arrived at the call centre to tell her of Terry's suicide. As soon as she saw her husband accompanied by a police officer she knew that Terry was dead. Her body experienced a severe physical reaction, her legs buckled, she collapsed to the floor and vomited.

In the days that followed his death, the DVD memory that played incessantly and invasively in Hilary's mind was the picture of her husband coming through the call centre doors with the police officer. She seemed unable to get this thought out of her mind and it seemed to be triggered by any memory of Terry. The only way that Hilary could cope was to try to banish all thoughts of Terry from her mind. She threw herself into her work, caring for her husband and her other children, re-decorating the house, doing anything that kept the memories of Terry quarantined in the box with a heavy weight on it.

The mind's immune system had provided Hilary with a short-term strategy to cope, but as time went on the strategy began to fail her. As she continued to use this method of coping she became more isolated from the rest of her family. Discussing Terry only served to play the DVD of his suicide, so whenever she could, she changed the topic of conversation. She had numbed her mind from the pain but in doing so, she was also unable to feel any joy or happiness. Hilary described herself as a zombie, outwardly going through the motions of life but emotionally dead inside.

By using some of the steps highlighted later in this book Hilary and I worked at gradually releasing the lid on the box so that she could grieve Terry properly. We gradually phased out the invasive negative memory of the night Terry died and replaced this with a very happy memory of Terry playing football as a child. Gradually Hilary accepted the fear, anger, sadness and sorrow and through this healing process she went on to make a positive contribution through a self-help group for other parents who had lost a child through suicide.

Summary of Chapter 7. Shock and awe.

The mind's immune system. When we experience emotionally difficult times the mind seems to have it's own immune system. The conscious mind is constantly on the lookout for potentially threatening situations because of its sensitivity to negative memories from the past that have been allowed through the filter from the sub-conscious mind.

The second aspect of the immune system analogy is with regard to especially traumatic life events that are very painful. In this instance it seems as if these particular DVD memories are placed in a box and a heavy weight is put on the lid. The box is then quarantined in a part of the mind's DVD library, never to be visited.

Keeping the lid on the box. By quarantining the box it is possible to avoid much of the fear, anger, sadness and sorrow that go with viewing this particular DVD. If we never watch the DVD we don't have to deal with the painful emotions. The problem seems to be that this can make us emotionally stunted. Unwilling or unable to deal with the negative emotions we become detached from being able to experience the positive emotions in life.

Lifting the lid off the box. By gradually lifting the lid off the box it is as if we release anti-bodies into our mind which help us gradually to play the painful DVD but to cope with the fear, anger, sadness and sorrow that initially accompanies the DVD. When we face up to our negative emotions we are able to feel more positive and hopeful about the future.

CHAPTER 8.
THE HABIT OF HAPPINESS.

The routes to depression.

Before we begin to discuss how we start to acquire the habit of happiness let's re-cap on the different routes to depression. People end up suffering from psychological distress for a variety of reasons. Firstly, some people have a predisposition to having their filter negatively set because their parents were very pessimistic abut life and they transferred this pessimism to their offspring through either their genes or from constantly reinforcing certain messages about how dangerous and difficult the world is. As I mentioned earlier, such people can become threat sensitive at quite a young age. The example of Daisy the sales woman describes this very well.

Alternatively, someone can acquire a predisposition to pessimism because they experienced a difficult childhood, which involved events that made them anxious about their immediate future. Lena's generalised anxiety over her intimidating father's moods describes this phenomenon.

The third possibility is that an individual may have experienced a very traumatic event either in childhood or adult life that resulted in their filter becoming set to notice negative DVD memories. Cathy's life reflects this: the traumas of her parent' separation, the rejection by both parents, being handed over to the care of her aunt and uncle and finally the sexual abuse she suffered at the hands of her uncle.

Finally, there are those people who are broadly optimistic who find themselves facing a difficult life event, or series of life events, which culminate in them temporarily re-setting their filter to notice the negative DVDs. A good example of this was John the newly promoted senior manager who was struggling to operate effectively in management meetings which he found very stressful.

In a sense it doesn't matter what the cause of the psychological distress is. A similar process is occurring in each of the routes to depression listed above. The filter has been set to allow negative DVDs from the sub-conscious to the conscious mind and it is the thinking errors that keep the filter in place. The effect of viewing these DVDs regularly over a period of time causes neuro-physiological changes in the neurotransmitters, particularly in the reduced levels of serotonin. The effect of viewing these DVDs is psychologically debilitating - self-doubt creeps in, confidence ebbs away and ultimately there is a loss of self –esteem which leads to negative self-fulfilling prophecies.

As I mentioned in Chapter 2 some of the chemical imbalances in women are a result of the physiological changes their bodies go through. This means that initially the driver for their depression may be primarily physiological rather than psychological, however, the two are very closely linked. If a woman suffering from postnatal depression has reduced levels of nor-epinephrine and serotonin the likelihood is that her filter will then become set to notice the negative aspects of her life.

It's probably true that the more traumatic the root cause in setting the filter to see the negative DVDs, and the longer the person has had their filter set in that position, then the more difficult it is to re-set the filter. In the last chapter we described the way the mind operates in situations where we suffer a real shock to our emotional system. After a powerfully traumatic incident some people find the process of re-setting the filter too painful and too much hard work. No technique comes with a guarantee of success. However, the techniques I'm going to describe in the next part of the book have enabled me to help hundreds of people to re-set their filters and live a happier life.

Practice makes permanent.
In his book, 'Psycho-cybernetics', Maxwell Maltz (1) suggests that happiness is a habit. There aren't any short cuts to beating psychological distress. The rest of 'The Promised Land' describes how to use certain strategies and techniques to help people to change their thinking. The thinking changes we need to make are to do with conquering the thinking errors. It's the thinking errors that hold the

filter in place which, in turn, allows the negative DVDs into our conscious mind and keeps the positive DVDs in our subconscious.

You can either let your mind control you, or you can control your mind; it's a fairly simple choice. The changes only come with practice. I liken it to physical training. If you decide you want to become physically fitter and you begin your training programme gradually, after a while you find you're able to do more and you also find that the training becomes easier. After several weeks or months you may have reached your desired level of fitness, but you can't stop training and hope that your fitness level will remain constant. However, if you keep up a certain level of training it becomes increasingly easier to fit it into your life. In fact, you start to miss it when you don't train. It's the same with positive thinking. If you regularly practice the strategies for making happiness a habit you will reap the benefits, but it requires effort and commitment – and that's something that only you can provide. The good news is that practice makes permanent – if you get into these good habits then this new way of thinking eventually marks a permanent change in your perception of life. You will find you become more balanced in your thinking and you will achieve the elusive equilibrium.

It's important to remember that this isn't about changing who you are as a person. In fact to a large degree it's the opposite: it's about accepting who you are but trying to change your perception of the situation so that you can fashion the situation to suit yourself. Psychologically healthy individuals are able to change their perception of their ability to handle their external world. Quite often the changes required are relatively minor. *Often it's no more than noticing the positive things that already exist in our external world.* Eleanor whose son Phillip had refused to go to school, pointed this out to me – "I'd spent so long focussing on the negative aspects of Phillip's behaviour, I'd stopped seeing what a great kid he is most of the time". When Eleanor changed her perception of Phillip she acted in a more positive way to him and not surprisingly, Phillip responded in a more positive way in return.

Good things are around us all the time, our filters simply don't allow them to make it from our sub-conscious mind to our conscious mind. The wonder of nature, small acts of kindness, beautiful music, the scent of flowers, children's laughter, overcoming life's little challenges, church bells, human touch - all of these can go unnoticed if we let them.

Success isn't a straight line upwards on the graph. The techniques described here take time to work, on average 6-12 weeks of regular practice depending on the severity of the thinking errors. You'll have good days and bad days, but the bad days don't cancel out the good days - the good days still happened and the positive DVD memories prove it!

Well Formed Outcomes (WFOs).
Practising the techniques that follow will help to address the thinking errors that lead us to making the negative assumptions, which filter the negative aspects of our world into our conscious mind. The first strategy focuses on the importance of getting clarity about what it is we want to achieve. Richard Bandler and John Grinder (2) noticed in their research on successful therapists that those therapists who were most effective asked their clients to define precisely what it was that they wanted to achieve from the therapy – a well formed outcome (WFO).

By doing this, two things happen. Firstly, it becomes possible to measure the progress being made on the journey to good psychological health. The clarity helps to do this – only by knowing the destination of the journey is it possible to estimate how far along the road we are. Secondly, being able to visualise what the destination looks like can be a powerful motivator in terms of helping us through the difficult parts of the journey. By using a notebook to record these WFOs (or indeed by using the appendix in this book) we are able to keep a written record, which can be used to assess our progress towards the outcomes.

There are seven questions that help to define more precisely what each person's outcomes might be:

1. "What outcomes do you want to achieve from this?"
   This is a very broad question but the greater the clarity the better. Some of the subsequent questions help to achieve greater clarity. There are no right or wrong answers to this question. However, remember that if you want to be able to measure your progress towards the outcome the more specific you are the easier it is to see how much progress you're making.

2. "Where, when and with who do you want to achieve your outcomes?"
   This helps to narrow down the focus. Sometimes people have a specific problem related to work, or it may be a confidence problem dealing with a specific group of people. Alternatively, it could be a relationship with one person that is troubling you. Putting a realistic time frame on achieving the outcome is important in helping to chart your progress. It's easy to get disheartened if you set yourself an unrealistically short timeframe. Often people have been struggling for many months, or even years, with their negative perception of the world. It's unrealistic to think that this perception might be turned around in just a couple of weeks.

3. "What will it look, sound and feel like when I've achieved my outcomes?"
   This type of visualisation can be very important in helping to motivate you when the effort seems too much. Having an attractive picture of what the future holds if your outcomes are achieved spurs most people on. Some people also benefit from thinking about what might happen if they *don't* manage to achieve their outcomes. A dark and miserable picture of a future with unachieved outcomes can be a sobering thought.

4. "Are you in control of the changes necessary to help you achieve your outcomes?"

   This is potentially a difficult question but it throws some light on what you can and can't control. It emphasises the balance on what you need to accept as opposed to what you need to change, and, consequently, where you should channel your energies.

5. "Will I lose anything if I succeed in achieving my outcomes?"

   There are often potential losses when people achieve their outcomes. Strange as it may sound, sometimes people even worry about losing their depression, especially if they've had it for a long time. Lena told me that sometimes she didn't want to let her husband know when she'd had a good day. She was worried that because she'd had one good day, he'd expect her to have a good day everyday and she wasn't sure she could cope with that pressure.

   On other occasions I've worked with people who have been trying to resolve troubled relationships or difficulties with regard to their job. The potential resolution of these stresses could mean the loss of a partner or deciding to look for a different job. Loss is a difficult concept because it has to be weighed against the potential gains, hence the next question.

6. "Is the outcome worth the effort?"

   If it isn't worth the effort you need to ask yourself some more questions. Are you really clear about the potential positive benefits of making the changes in your thinking? Do you understand the potential negative long-term consequences of not changing your thinking? If, on the other hand, the answer to this question is an unequivocal 'yes' and the outcome is worth the effort then don't cheat on how much honest effort you put into changing your thinking.

7. "What will all the positive consequences be of achieving my outcomes?"

List as many benefits that will emanate from being able to re-set your filter to notice all the positive things about you and your life. This may overlap with some of the other questions but that's a good thing – it reaffirms what you already know, that the outcome will be worth the effort.

The following extract is an example of one client's WFO. Alex was a nurse working in a busy Accident and Emergency (A&E) department in a large inner city hospital. She had been experiencing a number of life events over a six-month period. Her relationship of seven years had broken up and her ex-partner had left Alex with some financial problems. She had also suffered three bereavements in this time period, an uncle, her grandmother and a close work colleague. She described the combination of these events as "robbing her of the ability to cope with life." Alex was by nature a very caring person and this was true in her relationships outside work as well as being a major facet of her profession. It later transpired from the counselling that she felt an imbalance with her own needs – she spent more time caring for others than being cared for herself.

Alex was experiencing a number of symptoms – difficulty sleeping, feeling very lethargic, crying for no apparent reason, an inability to concentrate at work and she was becoming quite short tempered with colleagues and patients. Prior to this Alex described herself as resilient character who had worked in A&E for 11 years. Work had been the major stabilising influence in her life but she was now experiencing panic attacks and having difficulty making decisions at work as the self-doubt began to creep in.

Alex's line manager had noticed her problems at work and suggested she take some time off work to seek help. She had been to see her GP who had prescribed mild anti-depressants and referred Alex to me for counselling. At our first session I set Alex the task of developing her WFOs as her homework. This is what she produced.

1. "What outcomes do you want to achieve from this?"
   I want to get better, feel normal not depressed, I want to feel happy and stop crying. I want to be able to do my job as well as I used to, I want to get back to being Alex. I want to manage my stress and anxiety and increase my self-confidence. I want to be less selfless, I want a balance between caring for other people and caring for myself, I'd like to be able to talk openly about my feelings.
   Many of the things Alex mentions are not untypical – the desire to get back to where she was before she became depressed is very common. However, some of the things she mentions later are about taking her on a journey beyond simply going back to where she was before. Her outcomes are all quite concrete in the sense that she will be able to measure her progress towards the outcomes. It's easy to see the self-doubt and lack of confidence that has crept into Alex's mind as a result of viewing lots of negative DVDs. The thinking errors have arisen over her belief about her ability to cope and this is impacting on her ability, or her *perceived* ability to do her job well.

2. "Where, when and with who do you want to achieve your outcomes?"
   Now, as soon as possible! Over time I would like to be able to balance the good days with the bad days both at work and in my home life. I realise this will take a little time but I hope to achieve this in a few weeks.
   Whilst, like many people, she wants a quick end to her psychological distress, Alex has realised, that the therapeutic process will take some time. The time period of a few weeks isn't an unreasonable timeframe to challenge her thinking errors and re-set her filters given that she has been struggling for about six months.

3. "What will it look, sound and feel like when I've achieved my outcomes?"

I will be able to see and clarify exactly what is stressing me and I will be able to hear my own needs. I see myself dealing effectively and managing a range of stressful situations both at home and in my work. I will feel very balanced in the way I am dealing with problems. I am neither panicking nor pretending they don't exist.

Alex is clearly able to visualise what success looks, sounds and feels like. When I pressed her she was able to give me specific examples, particularly in the work situation. Despite the fact that I had only one session with Alex prior to her completing her WFOs, the theme of balance is coming through quite clearly, which we were able to pick up later in the counselling. The theme of balance can be related to balance in terms of both control and optimism (which were discussed earlier in the book). Her next answer also sheds some light on this.

4. "Are you in control of the changes necessary to help you achieve your outcomes?"
   Initially I didn't feel in control when I answered this question. I realise that the medication can help me in the short term but that it will compromise my control in the long term. I need to take charge of my life.
   Alex's response to this question is quite typical. The realisation has dawned on her that she has apparently lost control in some areas of her life. Alex also recognises that she needs to regain control wherever she can. As a health professional she was well aware of the short-term benefits that medication can offer, but was equally aware of the longer-term potential dependency associated with remaining on anti-depressants for long periods of time. We were able to process her thoughts on what can effect the symptoms i.e. the medication and what can effect the causes (the negative introspective thoughts) of her psychological distress.

5. "Will I lose anything if I succeed in achieving my outcomes?"

   My sanity if I don't! I will lose some of selflessness. Will I become more selfish? I will lose my self-doubt and become confident but does confident mean arrogant? Will I become an arrogant fool?

   Alex clearly recognises that she needs to achieve her outcomes in order to become well again. Her self-doubt is exemplified by her response to this question. She doesn't want to be seen as a selfish, arrogant person but it seems implicit that she understands that the balance needs to shift more towards addressing her own needs. Once again the concept of balance is coming through in her thinking. It's worth mentioning that many people who suffer from psychological distress find it difficult to get the balance between selflessness and selfishness. Later in the book I'll explain more about this balance.

6. "Is the outcome worth the effort?"

   Ultimately yes, but it's going to be a lot of hard work.

   Alex wasn't deluding herself about the amount of effort required to change her thinking and I was able to explore this further by getting her to expand on this answer.

7. "What will all the positive consequences be of achieving my outcomes?"

   I will feel well, I will not be an inconvenience to others, which is how I feel at the moment. I think my personality may change, I will become a more balanced person.

   This response gave us the opportunity to discuss what Alex needed to accept about herself i.e. certain fairly well defined aspects of her personality that won't change. We were also able to talk about how she could change the perception of both herself and the way she interacted with certain situations.

There are no right or wrong answers in WFOs, they simply offer an opportunity to help the client to explore their own thinking in terms of the concepts described in the earlier part of the book. You may find it helpful to write down your own WFOs in the appendix at the end of the book.

Positive Listing Exercise

It's important to remember that one of the main problems with depression is the sufferer's difficulty in playing any positive DVD memories because their filter is screening these out of their conscious mind. As the title of this chapter suggests, depressed people are out of the habit of playing memories that make them feel happy. So, with this in mind, the next exercise is to try to rekindle some of the happy memories from our previous experience of life. This exercise is aimed at encouraging people to dust off their positive DVDs and play these old favourites again.

I ask my clients to try to compile a written list of 20 positive memories. Often they feel overwhelmed by the idea of coming up with a list of so many positive memories because they are very out of practice. The solution to this is to try to do three a day for a week. By keeping this list in the same book as the WFOs, the list becomes a useful reference to help jog the positive memories when the negative memories start to weigh heavily. When you do this exercise, by keeping the book by your bedside and remembering to do three positive memories each night, you will find there are a number of benefits. Firstly, as we suggested earlier, it's easier to do the exercise in bitesize chunks. Secondly, the cumulative effect of little and often starts to become habit forming. Thirdly, playing these positive DVDs last thing at night can be a pleasant way to drop off to sleep and, because we are more in tune with our sub-conscious mind during sleep, it can also lead to sweeter dreams!

So what constitutes a positive DVD memory? It can be anything that induces a positive emotion by playing such a memory. For example, activities that you enjoy doing, achievements or qualifications, friends and family who love you, talents that you have, interesting experiences, wonderful days out, memorable holidays, meaningful pieces of work – anything that makes you feel positive.

As with WFOs there are no right or wrong answers. Below is a sample of the many and varied memories people have shared with me: Gardening; my cat; taking a hat trick in a cricket match when I was 18; my three children; swimming with dolphins on holiday; cooking a meal for friends; running a marathon; securing a successful business deal; my partner's smiling face; an evening out with work colleagues; getting a massage from my best friend; being on the beach with my kids; getting my degree; buying my house and making it into a home; walking my dog in the countryside.

The potential list is endless and by compiling such a list it gives us a ready made selection of positive DVDs that we can play when we start to feel distressed about our lives. Often depressed people find this exercise difficult to start. However, once they get into the exercise it's quite enjoyable and it becomes easier as one positive DVD seems to lead to another.

The point of the listing exercise is to deliberately get people back into the habit of thinking positively. By expressly asking them to trawl the shelves of their memory library we are getting them to practice the habit of happiness. In effect, the thinking errors are being challenged, the filter shifted and the positive memories pushed from the subconscious mind into the conscious mind.

By writing a list of positive memories in their notebook it helps people to see their lives, literally, through a different filter. Their levels of self-doubt decrease as they play DVDs of doing enjoyable activities that they have a talent for. The self-confidence starts to return when they think of their achievements and qualifications. They come to like themselves more and their self-esteem improves as they play the memories of family and friends who they have a mutual love and respect for.

Typically, most of the people I work with manage to come up with some very effective positive memories from their past life. However, often they comment on the fact that these memories are about the past rather than the present. Positive listing is a good exercise, but we need to take it a stage further. We need to bring the practice of looking for positive DVDs of the past into the present. If we can do this then we can start feeling more optimistic and hopeful about the future. To achieve this we need a different type of exercises, which will be covered in the next chapter.

Summary of Chapter 8. The habit of happiness.

The routes to depression. There are four basic routes to depression, all of them involve the sufferer's filter being set to filter negative DVDs from the sub-conscious into the conscious mind. Over time this leads to a pessimistic orientation. If this occurs early enough in life it can lead to some people having a predisposition to pessimism. The four routes are:

1. Having a parent(s) who worries about life and passes this worry on to their children.
2. Experiencing generalised anxieties in childhood. Both 1 and 2 can lead to early threat sensitivity.
3. Experiencing a traumatic event either in childhood or adult life can cause the filter to be set negatively in a very dramatic fashion.
4. Or, there are those people who are basically optimists but have had their filter gradually re-set to notice the negatives because they are experiencing one or more life events.

Practice makes permanent. The filter is kept in place by thinking errors and it's only by continually challenging the thinking errors that we are able to re-set the filters to start to allow more positive DVD thoughts into our conscious mind. It's hard work. There aren't any short cuts to challenging the thinking errors and it's like physical conditioning, if you stop challenging the thinking errors the negative filter will slip back in place. The good news is that very often you don't have to do anything else apart from challenging the thinking errors. Once the filter is adjusted we start to notice the good things that are already there in our lives.

Well Formed Outcomes. Clarity is very important in helping people who are suffering from psychological distress. By answering the seven questions to establish their WFOs, sufferers from psychological distress gain the clarity necessary to see what it is they want and what changes need to be made to get it. They can then identify the most pernicious thinking errors and can challenge these more effectively.

Positive Listing Exercise. The negative filter has operated for so long and so effectively that for many people they are simply out of practice in allowing the positive DVDs through the filter and into their conscious mind. By completing a positive list they begin to practice challenging the thinking errors and re-setting the filter.

CHAPTER 9.
THINKING MAKES IT SO.

As I mentioned at the end of the previous chapter the next stage is to progress from rekindling the memories of past positive experiences to envisioning a more hopeful, optimistic future. In order to do this we need to become more conscious of what is happening in the present, and in order to raise people's levels of consciousness about the present there are a number of exercises and concepts I use to help my clients.

Keeping a diary.
Hopefully my clients have got into the habit of writing things down in their books by now. So the next stage is to try to make them more consciously aware of their thinking in the present. I try to do this by encouraging them to use a diary. Once again it's an exercise best done at the end of the day on a regular basis in order to make their positive thinking more systematic – remember, practice makes permanent.

The instructions for keeping the dairy are quite simple. At the end of every day write down a few sentences to describe what happened over the course of the day. Then rate the day in terms of how it felt: 1 = It was a terrible day to 10 = It was a fantastic day.
Then read the list of thinking errors to see if you are making any negative assumptions which, if successfully challenged, will prove to be false. As a result of the successful challenges the scores often improve.

Recording the thoughts and feelings as they occur is a powerful way of helping to do a number of things. It allows us to make comparisons between days, we can track patterns to see whether there are certain triggers that cause us to score certain days higher or lower than others. Most importantly though, it gives us a chance to challenge our thinking errors as they occur.

If the scores are consistently low this may be due to certain thinking errors locking the filter in place so that the positive memories of the day are stuck in the subconscious mind. The example below shows how effective Martin's thinking errors were at locking the filter in place. The thinking error he was making on this particular day was to disqualify a positive experience.

Martin came from a large family with seven brothers and sisters. He was currently experiencing a number of life events: the premature death of one of his brothers: a terminally ill sister; the recent break up of a relationship; and he had also been involved in a car crash, which had rocked his confidence. It wasn't a case of a little rain falling in Martin's life, it was a monsoon! After doing his WFOs and positive listing exercise, I set Martin the task of keeping a diary and rating each day.

At our next session Martin was recounting a particularly low scoring day – which he had rated as a 2. He described how stressed he'd felt at work because he was focussed on the support he had to give his terminally ill sister and the fact that he didn't want to drive to a sales meeting for fear of crashing the car. He also commented on the sadness he felt over the fact that he had no emotional support in dealing with these issues. As soon as he got home he had a difficult phone call from his deceased brother's partner about some legal issues that had arisen because his brother had died without making a will.

Martin felt thoroughly depressed and his rating of 2 for this particular day reflected this. I noticed that Martin hadn't commented in his diary on what he'd done that evening. When I asked him what he'd done that evening, he closed his eyes and started to play the DVD memory. After he'd located the memory in his library he nodded his head and then smiled. "Actually I went to choir practice that evening." He then recounted his attendance at a male voice choir practice. He had enjoyed the singing and the camaraderie of going for a drink and a bite to eat afterwards. I asked him why he hadn't written about it in his diary. His reply was "Well it doesn't really count."

On further gentle probing it appeared that Martin felt it was somehow wrong to acknowledge anything positive in his life because he had to focus on the more pressing negative events he was dealing with. Finally I asked him "Taking into account the choir practice, how would you rate the day retrospectively?" Martin thought for a while and eventually said "Well taking the evening into account as well, the day as a whole would have rated at least a five."

Diary keeping is excellent practice at challenging the thinking errors. To paraphrase Shakespeare, "no day is a bad day but thinking makes it so." Even on our most difficult days good things happen but they just get filtered out. Re-set the filter and the good things are noticed. When we notice the good things this improves the way we rate the day.

Visualisation.
Diary keeping is effective at helping to gradually adjust the filters. However, sometimes people have particularly sad and painful DVD memories that have the potential to dominate our thinking. In dealing with these we may need a different technique. As we mentioned earlier one of the ways we try to cope with very powerful negative memories is to place them in a box on a shelf at the back of the mind's library with a heavy weight on the box to make the sure the lid doesn't fly off. The problem with this approach is that we are acutely aware of the presence of this box in our mind's library. Even if we don't open the box, we still know it's there with all the painful memories stowed inside.

In order to exorcise the negative feelings of these painful memories we need to gradually open the box. Slowly confronting the anger, fear, sadness and sorrow, particularly with the help of a counsellor can be very effective in reducing the power of these DVDs to hurt us. After a time we learn to forgive all the parties involved in these painful events – including ourselves.

John Gray (1) in his book provides many exercises to help people try to take the lid off the box and start to view the DVDs through a more positive filter. Many of the exercises are designed specifically to deal with coming to terms with the painful loss of a relationship. Most of the exercises are effective in trying to change the filters around to look at some of the more positive aspects of the relationship. The more positive our view is of all the parties involved in the breakdown of a relationship then the easier it is to heal the pain.

Despite the effectiveness of the exercises outlined in John Gray's book there isn't anything specifically designed to help open the box when the contents are very traumatic and the DVD memories invoke extreme emotional reactions. Visualisation is a technique that can be used to help people who find that certain memories are so powerful that they are prevented from being able to address the thinking memories in the normal way we've described.

One of my clients, Chloe had been involved in a road rage incident where another motorist had stopped his car, verbally abused her and then assaulted her. Chloe had been a fairly positive person before this incident and she had also been a confident driver. Her job in Social Services involved visiting people in their homes and required her to drive throughout the district in which she worked. After the road rage incident Chloe lost her confidence and was reluctant to drive anywhere that was unfamiliar. She panicked every time she got in the car and if another driver looked at her or sounded their horn she would burst into tears regardless of who the horn was directed at.

Chloe was still deeply troubled by the intrusive DVD memories that would invade her mind after being triggered by a cue such as a car horn being sounded aggressively or the sight of a similar car to the one driven by her attacker. The DVD memory itself was getting in the way of challenging the thinking errors that were keeping the negative filter in place. Until we were able to deal with the intrusive negative thoughts which caused Chloe to panic it would remain difficult to help Chloe move on.

Together we used a visualisation technique for helping to dilute the power of the memory. I reproduce the technique here in a general format, which can be used effectively in two scenarios. Firstly where a negative memory is triggered by a specific cue that is causing the sufferer an inability to allow them to confront the thinking error. Chloe's example above falls into this category. She became so panicky when certain cues reminded her of the road rage incident that she was unable to think rationally about challenging any of her thinking errors.

Secondly, this type of technique can be used where the thinking error has been successfully confronted but is still triggered on occasions by an unidentified cue. An example of this would be a client of mine called Steven who occasionally suffered flashbacks about a time when a very domineering manager bullied him at work. Although Steven had moved on tremendously in terms of challenging his thinking errors, unaccountably he would occasionally get very vivid memories of one particularly painful meeting with his manager.

In order to utilise this technique we need two DVD memories, the negative one which is causing the problem and a very positive unrelated DVD memory. The positive memory should preferably be one in which you feel empowered, in control and confident. The technique involves taking the negative memory and deliberately changing the modalities in the memory. We literally change what we see, hear and feel in the memory as if it were a DVD being shown on a TV screen, the power of the negative memory is thus diluted. We can then link the negative memory to the positive memory, which we enhance by changing the modalities to make the positive memory even more vibrant and exciting. This has the effect of making the negative memory the cue for triggering the positive memory.

This is how the technique works. Take the negative DVD and begin to watch it with your eyes closed, but imagine that you are watching the DVD on a TV screen for which you have a special remote control. As you are watching the DVD note the different colours in the DVD and use the remote control to turn the colours to black and white. Once you have changed it into a black and white film, use the remote to turn the sound all the way down until it's become a silent film. Watch the people in the film saying things without any sounds coming out of their mouths. Then turn the film into slow motion so all the characters look quite surreal in their movements. As you are watching the DVD become aware of the air temperature in the scene being shown on the screen, adjust the temperature either up or down so that it is radically different to your actual memory. At this point adjust the contrast so that the quality of the picture becomes very poor and the screen appears to have a snowstorm effect, notice how the clarity of the images become gradually less and less distinct. Finally press a button on the remote control that shrinks the film down to a white dot in the centre of the screen. Mentally move this dot to one corner of the screen, for example top left, then press another button on the remote control.

This time the screen is filled by a very positive DVD. As you watch the images in this DVD note all the colours and adjust the colour to make the colours as bright and vivid as possible. Enjoy looking at the deep colours and then tune the sound in so that it's wonderfully clear without being loud, imagine the sound is in stereo, perhaps there is a favourite musical soundtrack accompanying the images. You can see all the detail on the faces of the people in this positive DVD and you can hear their voices clearly. Adjust the temperature in the scene using the remote control so that it is wonderfully ambient, not too hot or too cool. Then make the images as sharp as possible by adjusting the contrast. Finally at the most positive point in the film freeze the frame and admire the picture you've just created in wonderful technicolour and listen to the beautiful soundtrack.

Now 'anchor' this positive picture to two things. Firstly anchor the picture to a word or phrase that you say out loud to yourself. Secondly anchor the picture to an unobtrusive, yet unusual gesture such as squeezing your little finger. Look at the picture, concentrate hard on it and say the word and make the gesture.

Then press the button on the remote control and shrink the picture down to a dot. Mentally place the dot in another corner of the screen, for example the bottom right. Then go to the 'negative' dot in the top left of the screen and bring it to the centre of the screen, open up the negative dot and run the DVD picture. Repeat the process of making the DVD black and white, silent, in slow motion, with the temperature changed before creating the snowstorm effect and shrinking it to the dot, which is placed back in the top left corner of the screen.

Go to the bottom right and use the remote control to bring the positive dot to the centre of the screen and run the positive DVD. Repeat the process of enhancing the colours, giving it a soundtrack, adjusting the temperature, sharpening the images, freezing the frame and anchoring the picture to the spoken phrase or word and the physical gesture. Shrink the picture down and return it to the bottom right corner of the screen.

Repeat the same process once more with each DVD.

This technique attempts to do a number of things utilising some powerful elements of neurolinguistic programming, NLP (2). One of the main tenets of NLP suggests that we think by using our three most predominant senses - visual (pictures), auditory (sound) and kinaesthetic (feelings). By using these modalities we can dilute the negative DVDs and enhance the positive DVDs very effectively. Anthony Robbins (3) has written extensively in greater depth how NLP techniques can be harnessed in this way.

As I mentioned earlier, the negative DVDs can sometimes pop into our heads for no apparent reason. They can be triggered by a cue such as something we see, hear, touch, smell or taste. So subtle are these triggers that we may not even be aware of them at the time because they operate at a subconscious level.

In chapter two, I mentioned Maureen who moved from one place of work to another but found herself inexplicably playing negative DVD memories of her old stressful job, despite the fact that she was at her new place of work. Eventually she worked out that it was the smell of the floor cleaner that was operating as the sub-conscious trigger for playing the negative DVDs.

So, we may not be able to prevent the memories from coming into our minds, however, by practising the technique of diluting the negative memory it strips the DVD of it's power to cause us such discomfort. Secondly we then use the negative DVD itself as the cue to trigger the positive DVD by connecting the two closely together. Finally we anchor the positive DVD to a spoken word or phrase and a physical gesture. The more we practice this then the greater our ability to run the positive DVD effortlessly by 'firing' the anchors of the word/phrase and gesture. The advantage of this is that if we find ourselves in a difficult situation where the negative DVDs start to play, we can activate the positive DVD by saying the word or phrase to ourselves whilst at the same time using the gesture.

Using the power of the mind to help both overcome painful negative memories and enhance positive memories is a very effective way of ensuring that the positive DVDs are the closest to hand in our mental DVD library.

I used this technique very effectively with Steven in the example I mentioned earlier in this chapter. Steven was a senior hospital administrator. He had been through a painful separation from his wife and young daughter and the consequent cycle of thinking errors, filter, self-doubt, lack of confidence and low self-esteem had affected him significantly. His self-esteem was also being eroded by his relationship with a very authoritative manager, Patricia whom he seemed to be in conflict with over many administrative matters. The situation had come to a head one day when he and Patricia had a very strong disagreement where Steven had felt publicly humiliated. Steven felt so down about things that he sought the advice of the Occupational Health Dept who signed him off sick from work and referred him to me.

Over a few weeks together we worked through our WFOs, positive listings and the diary/thinking error exercise. Steven was almost ready to return to work on a gradual rehabilitation programme but the thought of having to work with Patricia again caused him great anxiety. In order to combat this we used the visualisation technique described above.

The negative DVD that was causing the anxiety was the memory of Patricia's public humiliation of Steven. We worked on this DVD to dilute its power to make Steven feel anxious. We also needed a positive DVD from Steven's memory library to enhance his feeling of confidence and self-esteem to use as his anchor. Steven had previously served in the Navy as a medical orderly. He had seen active service and had successfully worked in battle station conditions treating wounded service men in very stressful conditions. We utilised one such memory of him remaining calm and confident in the midst of chaos. He used the phrase "action stations" and the gesture of rubbing the back of his neck whilst saying the phrase out loud to himself every time we repeated the visualisation exercise.

On his first day back at work Steven had to attend a meeting with Patricia. He later told me that as he sat down with her he began to feel the anxiety rise as the negative memory of the public humiliation surfaced. He began to gently rub the back of his neck and mentally said the phrase "action stations" to himself. As he did so this triggered the positive DVD and the consequent feelings of confidence and self-esteem. To this day, whenever Steven feels anxious about a situation he fires his anchor and is able to recreate the positive emotions evoked by this positive DVD.

Visualisation can of course be used to simply enhance positive images of the past without the involvement of diluting a negative image. It can be used to help us relax, to promote feelings of self-confidence and, by visualising future events, we increase the likelihood of positive self-fulfilling prophecies. If we can see, hear and feel what a successful outcome is like we can programme our mind so that our body delivers the successful outcome.

Summary of Chapter 9. Thinking makes it so.

Keeping a diary. As a client becomes more aware of how their filter is working, keeping a diary enables them to raise their levels of consciousness about what type of thoughts are being registered in their conscious mind. Using the diary helps to challenge the thinking errors. By asking people to rate their day from 1 – 10 this encourages them to challenge the validity of low scores to see whether the scores reflect the thinking errors which have locked the negative filter in place and caused the positive aspects that occurred during the day to remain unnoticed.

Visualisation.
Using the power of the mind to help overcome painful negative memories and enhance positive memories is a very effective way of ensuring that the positive DVDs are the closest to hand in our mental DVD library. Visualisation is particularly effective when a memory is so powerful that it hinders our ability to challenge the thinking errors. Diluting the power of the memory allows us to start challenging the thinking errors. Linking the negative memory to a positive memory makes the negative memory a cue that triggers the positive memory. Using a phrase and gesture to anchor the positive DVD memory allows the feelings of confidence and self-esteem to be accessed very effectively.

CHAPTER 10.
MOVE ON UP.

As my clients begin to find that they are dealing more and more effectively with thinking errors they become well versed in the habit of happiness. This is the time when they have the opportunity to grow and develop even further, but we need a subtly different kind of thinking to take us on to the next level. Planning ahead becomes very important, but perhaps even more important is the idea of taking risks. Risk – the currency of the gods - is the enemy of threat sensitive people. As we mentioned earlier in the book, most people who are suffering from psychological distress are either predisposed to, or have temporarily become, threat sensitive. This inhibits their ability to grasp opportunities that appear to have an element of risk attached. To move people onwards to the Promised Land we need to move through certain stages of threat sensitivity and this chapter offers some suggestions of how to do this.

The importance of play.
Earlier in the book when I spoke of the cause of depression I mentioned that there were two facets to it. Firstly the negative introspection, and secondly the lack of participation in pleasure giving activities. It's easy to see how the two combine to lead people into a depressive cycle. When our conscious mind is fed a steady diet of negative DVDs via the filter, the consequent self-doubt and lack of confidence means we often stop engaging in activities which give us pleasure. Re-establishing some of these behaviours is the first step to moving on up.

Eleanor told me how she used to go to the gym at least 3 or 4 times a week before she became depressed. However, when she was struggling to cope with her son Phillip's behaviour she started to lose her confidence. She stopped going to one of her favourite aerobics classes at the gym because she began to doubt her ability to follow the instructors' moves correctly. One of the main reasons she enjoyed the gym previously was that she felt it kept her in good physical shape. Eleanor had previously had difficulty keeping her weight down. As her lack of confidence transcended into low self-esteem she also began to feel very self-conscious about wearing figure-hugging outfits in the gym. Eventually she stopped going despite the fact that her physical appearance was suffering as she began to put weight on. The weight gain provided her with yet another negative DVD which made her feel more depressed and lowered her self esteem even further. This is a classic example of how the two elements of depression combined to trap Eleanor in her depressive cycle – the negative introspection and the lack of participation in an enjoyable activity.

If we are suffering from psychological distress it becomes even more important to take part in activities which give us some pleasure. The type of activity is not important, although there is quite a long history of research, including some of my own studies (1) which suggest that physical activity is particularly helpful in combatting stress. One of the homework activities I give to my clients as they start to progress is to set them a target of completing one or two of their favourite activities each week. It takes a big effort to overcome the inertia. Suffering from psychological distress is often energy draining which is another facet of the debilitating cycle. However, recalling question six from the WFOs usually focuses my clients' minds – "Is the outcome worth the effort?" Jointly agreeing which activity they will take part in before our next session helps to overcome the inertia.

As I mentioned earlier, the activity can take any form as long as it gives the individual some pleasure. Gardening, playing the piano, dancing along to the radio, horse riding, reading, swimming, walking, painting are all examples of activities that people I have worked with have chosen as their homework. By engaging in an enjoyable activity it breaks the negative cycle and usually provides the individual with a positive DVD of their day to counter some of the negative thoughts.

Proper Selfishness.
One of the reasons why many clients struggle to overcome the inertia is that they feel very guilty about putting themselves first. The guilt emanates from the thinking error on 'should statements'. It particularly effects clients who are off work suffering from psychological distress. They feel that they *shouldn't* be doing things that they enjoy because

taking part in pleasurable activities appears inconsistent with being off sick from work with anxiety, stress or depression. Many people also feel that spending time engaging in such positive activities is time that *should* be spent doing other things, such as caring for their family or doing household chores. However, people experiencing these types of psychological distress actually need to put themselves first in order to re-charge their batteries. This is the concept of 'proper selfishness'.

The writer Charles Handy (2) coined this phrase and it seems to be a very pertinent phrase when it comes to the importance of play. A good analogy of proper selfishness comes from the safety talk given by the cabin crew to passengers on an aeroplane flight. The crew instructs passengers that if the cabin pressure drops, oxygen masks will be released from the overhead compartment. Passengers are then told that if they are travelling with someone who needs their care, they should put their *own* mask on first so that they will then be able to look after the person in their care.

Barbara was a single parent who had been struggling with depression for several weeks. Although we had addressed the thinking errors and begun to adjust the filter she still spent most of her time working, looking after her two teenage children and keeping up with the chores around the house at weekends. At one of her sessions she wistfully recalled how she used to enjoy horse riding many years ago. I asked her why she didn't take up this activity again. Initially she gave me a raft of reasons ranging from the cost to not having enough time. All the reasons were rooted in putting other people first. After we processed each reason together, and we discussed the concept of proper selfishness, Barbara eventually agreed to go horse riding as her homework.

At the next session she recalled how, having booked a ride earlier in the week, she had got up on Saturday morning and told her children that she was going riding and would return in two hours. On driving to the riding school she felt very guilty that she was spending time on herself when she could have been doing household chores or engaging in some kind of activities with her children.

Having managed to recall our discussion on proper selfishness she was able to enjoy her ride and when she arrived home two hours later she recounted how much more energy she had for the chores and how much less resentful she was at having to do them. Putting herself first recharged her depleted energy levels. Taking part in an activity she was good at increased her levels of confidence. Recognising that she was important enough to sometimes put herself first improved her self-esteem.

The next stage in moving towards the Promised Land is to decide how you can use the concept of proper selfishness to enhance your own life. Find an appropriate activity that you enjoy and have a talent for, then make a commitment to spending some time regularly engaging in this activity.

Thinking ahead – Viking Behaviour.
Being spontaneous is something that people who are suffering from psychological distress find difficult. Planning enjoyable activities well ahead appears to work far better and I believe this is largely due to the fact that by planning ahead we create positive DVDs about the future. This has a beneficial effect in countering the negative thoughts and a bright picture of the future can help motivate us when we are trying to cope with difficult times in the present. Anticipation is part of the enjoyment. Being spontaneous, on the other hand, not only lacks the anticipation, it also requires a level of confidence which is probably not yet at hand for those suffering from psychological distress. So, thinking ahead and making plans is a very worthwhile exercise.

My experience of counselling clients with depression is that often they feel they don't have anything to look forward to in their lives. Their filters don't allow them to notice the positive things in their present lives so it becomes very difficult for them to imagine that there might be anything positive about the future. Planning ahead helps us to create a bright future. But how do we develop the confidence to take risks when there is only a short window of opportunity? Risk taking is the next stage in overcoming the threat sensitive behaviour driven by the thinking errors and the negatively set filter.

Often my clients struggle with the idea of taking what they perceive as a big risk. One of my clients, Jim, had been a laboratory technician for 25 years. At 18, his girlfriend became pregnant and much to the disappointment of his parents he decided to marry her and give up the opportunity to go to University to study electrical engineering. He started work as a laboratory technician to support his wife and child but unfortunately the marriage didn't last and after 10 years, and two more children, Jim got divorced. Jim carried on working as laboratory technician and was promoted to become the manager of the laboratory. He eventually got re-married to a nurse, and although she had two children there was a possibility that Jim could go back to University to study electrical engineering. However, Jim was worried that the family finances would be extremely stretched. He was also concerned that if he gave up his job he would lose the security of the pension scheme and the perks of his seniority. Most of all though, he was frightened that if he failed at University he would be unable to get his old job back.

At the same time, Jim was becoming increasingly frustrated with his work and his performance had started to deteriorate. His relationship with his boss was quite poor and they often seemed to clash over relatively minor issues. This situation had been ongoing for several months and it culminated in Jim being given an official warning. Jim was becoming increasingly stressed and anxious about work and had been prescribed anti-depressants by his doctor. He was experiencing a subtle juxtaposition – on the one hand he didn't want to leave his safe, secure job, but on the other hand he felt chained to a job which was 'depriving' him of the opportunity to launch a new career.

Having listened to Jim describe his frustrations over several sessions we began to make some progress. He was fairly clear in his own mind that going to University was the right choice for him. However, he was having great difficulty making the final decision; he still saw it as a big risk. As his confidence started to increase I mentioned the concept of 'Viking behaviour'.

Legend has it that many years ago when the Vikings invaded the North of England the Viking leader commanded his men to pull their long boats onto the shore and set fire to them. By getting them to burn their boats the Viking commander believed that it would force his men to fight much harder in the knowledge that there was no possibility of retreating to their boats and sailing back to Scandinavia. By burning their boats they also sent a very clear message to the enemy – the Vikings mean business.

When I finished my story it was the end of Jim's session and he told me he would continue to give his predicament some more thought for our next meeting. When Jim returned the following week, he handed me a piece of paper to read. It was his resignation letter. He explained that having pondered the concept of Viking behaviour he realised that he needed to make a really clear decision because this would force him to think about his future in a different way with a different attitude. By giving his employer three months notice this allowed him to finalise his university place, make some adjustments to his financial position and give his employer a reasonable timeframe to recruit a replacement. Going to university was a risk, but he felt that he was managing the risk as well as he could by putting it into a three-month time frame.

Jim had done two things. Firstly, he had made a firm decision in order to drive his thinking forward into the future and adjust his attitude accordingly. Secondly, he had given himself a period of time to adjust for the changes and to plan and prepare for his future change of direction. A few months later I heard how much Jim was enjoying his electrical engineering course and how he was looking forward to starting a new career.

Summary of Chapter 10. Move on up

The Importance of Play. The second strand of depression is the lack of participation in pleasure giving activities. When it is combined with negative introspection it drags people into a cycle which is self-perpetuating. Repeated negative introspection leaves people feeling drained and unable to take part in activities. By not taking part in activities they enjoy, the sufferer has fewer positive DVDs with which to challenge the thinking errors. Engaging in pleasure giving activities is the first step forward into the future.

Proper Selfishness. Part of the problem with not taking part in enjoyable activities is that sufferers from depression, anxiety and stress often feel guilty at the thought of putting themselves first. The concept of proper selfishness means that if, on occasions, they put themselves first they re-charge their own batteries and, consequently, others benefit from this.

Thinking Ahead – Viking Behaviour. Planning enjoyable activities and thinking ahead is a useful way of creating a bright future. Having 'something to look forward to' is actually an enjoyable experience in itself because of the pleasurable anticipation. We can create positive DVDs about the future and this helps us to deal with difficult situations in our present. However, some future opportunities appear quite risky. Threat sensitive people are often risk averse so finding a way for people to take risks but also to manage the risk effectively becomes important. The concept of Viking behaviour recognises that once people have made a decision it drives a very different, more positive way of thinking about the risks – burning your boats.

EPILOGUE
BEACH GLASS

Hopefully, through the concepts in this book I've been able to lead you along the way to the Promised Land. Our journey started out by explaining that psychological distress seems to be much more prevalent in the 21st century because we have greater expectations that our higher level motivational needs should be met. We then introduced the concept of the library full of DVDs in our mind that represents the memory bank of our experiences of life. The increased prevalence of anxiety, stress and depression is linked to the fact that we may have an increasing number of negative DVDs in our library. We talked about the filter, which is set to notice the negative DVDs and the thinking errors that keep the filter firmly in place. From this we noted that self-doubt creeps in as we are constantly fed negative images of our lives and ourselves - this leads to low self-esteem, which in turn can eventually lead to negative self-fulfilling prophecies.

We then spent some time looking at the way we interact with our external world, the match between our values, traits and styles and the life events we experience. Our deliberations then turned to why some people may be more susceptible to stress, anxiety and depression because of a tendency towards threat sensitivity, which is often developed early in life. We also touched on fundamental attribution error and noted how people often attach too much blame to themselves (or others) without giving sufficient regard to the circumstances they find themselves in.

The next milestone on our journey was the concept of control and the lesson we learned here was to accept that we can only control our own behaviour. We need to channel our energies into controlling what we can and letting go of what we can't. We also recognised the need to balance pessimism and blind optimism through the Stockdale paradox, when times are tough we must face up to the brutal truth but remain optimistic that we will eventually overcome our difficulties.

We spent a little time exploring the idea of the mind's immune system and how it tries to quarantine very shocking and painful DVD memories by isolating them in a box. We talked about how important it is to lift the lid on the box in order to dilute the power these particular negative memories hold over us.

As we moved towards the latter stages of our journey we discussed exercises specifically designed at helping to practice more positive thinking so that we can begin to eradicate the thinking errors. Well-formed outcomes highlight the importance of clear goals whilst the positive listing exercise provides a ready-made store of positive DVDs. Diary keeping makes us more consciously aware of our thoughts each day and visualisation can be a powerful mechanism for eradicating negative memories, enhancing positive memories and visualising a bright future.

Finally, our journey ended by outlining how important it is to take part in enjoyable activities and, in order to do this, why we should sometimes put ourselves first – proper selfishness. The last concept we touched upon was Viking behaviour, which helps us to think ahead and grasp opportunities to make a better, more fulfilling life.

Life is not for the fainthearted - into every life a little rain must fall. However, by understanding the concepts mentioned above and by practising positive thinking we can become more confident in our ability to create our own Promised Land. As Bob Marley once observed – 'If you knew what life was worth, you would find yours here on earth'. Despite the trials and tribulations, it's still a wonderful world. Which is why I'm so fond of beach glass......

I was born in the city of Portsmouth and spent many happy hours as a child playing on Southsea beach with my brother, sisters and cousins. Southsea beach is a pebble beach and the coastal waters of the English Channel relentlessly roll in on the tides every day of the year.

As kids we were always interested in different shaped pebbles and shells and the various items of flotsam and jetsam washed up by the tide. My own treasure from the beach was, and still is, beach glass. Sometimes glass bottles get washed up on the shore and the waves smash the bottle against the pebbles. Over the years the glass gets broken into fragments and these pieces of glass get churned up with the pebbles as the tides roll in and out each day.

Over the years the glass has its sharp edges worn down until they become smooth. Instead of its original transparency the glass gets marked by a million scratches, which create a wonderful translucent effect. It is transformed from a sharp clear shard of glass into a beautiful translucent pebble.

I believe this is a metaphor for how we go through life. We start out like a sharp, clear shard of broken glass. The tide of life washes us daily against a myriad of different pebble like experiences and over the years these experiences make their mark upon us, both physically and emotionally. Some of those experiences are happy and joyful, some are sad and painful. We carry the scars and the laughter lines on our bodies and the memories are indelibly etched upon our minds.

Each one of us, like every piece of beach glass, is unique and beautiful; and it is how we deal with our life experiences that make us so.

……..and finally, an appeal on behalf of children who may not have a Promised Land ahead of them without some help from us.

Let The Children Live!
P.O. Box 11
WALSINGHAM
Norfolk
NR22 6EH

They are called "the disposable ones", the children who live - and sometimes die – in the streets and the rubbish dumps of the cities of Colombia in South America. These *gamines* range from six-year-olds to teenagers, they are often unloved, unwanted, beaten, robbed, abused, raped and murdered.

Although the Colombians are generally a kind and generous people, crime related to the cocaine traffic has made cities like Medellin amongst the most violent in the world. In the poverty and squalor of the shantytowns, families tend to disintegrate and many children find themselves alone on the street.

They have to survive as best they can, but they easily fall prey to violence and abuse. Many of the street children sniff glue as an escape from the pain, hunger and loneliness.

Let the Children Live is a small registered charity with an enormous and vital task to perform: saving and transforming the lives of as many street-children as possible, and to prevent other children from having to take to the streets at all. Quite simply, the more funds they can raise, the more children they can reach – and the fewer gamines will be 'disposed of'.

A percentage of the profits from the sale of this book are going to support Let the Children Live, however, if everyone who reads this book made a contribution to this charity we could make a tremendous difference to the lives of so many children. Please help by making a gift or a banker's order by completing the form on the following page. Let's create a Promised Land for the gamines.

Thank you for your kindness, Rick

Further copies of this book can be obtained online from authorhouse.co.uk or from Amazon. co.uk or by order from Waterstones.

My Gift

Title: The Rev' d/Dr/Mr/Mrs/Miss ——————

Name: ....

Address: ....

....

—————————— *Postcode:* ——————

☐ I enclose my Cheque/Postal Order for £ ——————

☐ Please debit my VISA/MasterCard for £ ——————

Account No. ☐☐☐☐☐☐☐☐☐☐☐☐☐☐☐☐

Expires: ———————— *Signature:* ——————————

☐ I pay U.K. Income Tax and wish to make this donation under the Gift Aid Scheme.

☐ I do **not** require a receipt.   *THANK YOU!*

Banker's Order

To the Manager, *(Name of Bank)* ——————————

(Address of Bank) ——————————————

—————————— *(Postcode)* ——————

Please pay **Let The Children Live!** Account No. 20-20-15 60932469 at Barclays Bank, 128, High Street, Cheltenham, GL50 1EL

the sum of £ ———— on the ———— day of———— 20 ——

and on the same day each year/month* until further notice from

my Account No. ——————————————

Name of Account: ——————————————

Address: ——————————————

——————————————

—————————— *(Postcode)* ——————

Signature: —————————— Date: ——————

* Delete as appropiate
Let The Children Live! is Registered Charity No. 1013634

A gift from a reader of The Promised Land.

APPENDIX 1
WELL FORMED OUTCOMES.

1. "What outcomes do you want to achieve from this?"
This is a very broad question but the greater the clarity the better. Some of the subsequent questions help to get greater clarity. There are no right or wrong answers to this question, however, remember that if you want to be able to measure your progress towards the outcome the more clarity you have the easier it is to see how much progress you're making.

2. "Where, when and with who do you want to achieve your outcomes?"
This helps to narrow down the focus. Sometimes people have a specific problem related to work for example or it may be a confidence problem dealing with a specific group of people. Putting a realistic time frame on achieving the outcomes can also help chart your progress.

3. "What will it look, sound and feel like when I've achieved my outcomes?"

This type of visualisation can be very important in helping to motivate you when the effort seems too much. Having an attractive picture of what the future holds spurs people on to achieve their outcomes.

4. "Are you in control of the changes necessary to help you achieve your outcomes?"

This is potentially a difficult question but it does throw some light on what you can and can't control, what you need to accept Vs what you need to change, and where you should channel your energies.

5. "Will I lose anything if I succeed in achieving my outcomes?"
Loss is a difficult concept because it has to be weighed against the potential gains, hence the next question.

6. "Is the outcome worth the effort?"
If it isn't you need to ask some more questions. Are you really clear about the potential positive benefits of making the changes in your thinking? Do you understand the potential negative long-term consequences of not changing your thinking? If, on the other hand, the answer to this question is an unequivocal 'yes' the outcome is worth the effort then don't cheat on how much honest effort you put into changing your thinking.

7. "What will all the positive consequences be of achieving my outcomes?"

List as many benefits that will emanate from you being able to re-set your filter to notice all the positive things in your life. This may overlap with some of the other questions but that's a good thing – it reaffirms what you already know, that the outcome will be worth the effort.

APPENDIX 2
POSITIVE LISTING EXERCISE.

1.

2.

3.

4.

5.

6.

7.

8.

9.

10.

11.

12.

13.

14.

Dr. Rick Norris

15.

16.

17.

18.

19.

20.

References.

Introduction.
1. Glasser, W. 1998. Choice Theory. Harper Perennial.

Chapter 1.
1. Schwartz, J. Workplace Stress: Americans' Bugaboo. 2004. New York Times, September 5, p.D2.
2. Maslow, A. A theory of human motivation. 1942. Psychological Review vol 50 pp 370 – 396.
3. Clegg, S. 1999. Modern Organisations. Sage.
4. Glasser, W. 1998. Choice Theory. Harper Perennial.
5. Tam, H. 1998. Communitarianism. Macmillan Press.
6. Chartered Institute of Personnel and Development website 12.6.2005
7. Confederation of British Industry Statistics. 2004.
8. UK Office for National Statistics. 2005.

Chapter 2.
1. Psychology Today. March 1999.
2. US National Institute of Health Publication Number 00-4501 1999 reprinted 2000.

Chapter 3.
1. Burns D. Feeling Good. 1980. The new mood therapy. Avon Paperbacks. 1980.

Chapter 4.
1. Buckingham M and Clifton D. Now discover your strengths. Simon and Schuster. 2002
2. Robbins A. Unlimited Power. 1986. Simon and Schuster Ltd. Reprinted 2001.

Chapter 5.
1. Rath T and Clifton D. 2004. How full is your bucket? Gallup Press.
2. Seligman MEP and Schulman P. 1986. Explanatory style as

a predictor of productivity and quitting among life insurance agents. Journal of Personality and Social Psychology 50, 832 – 838.
3. Jones EE and Harris VA. 1967. The attribution of attitudes. Journal of Experimental Social Psychology 3, 1 – 24.
4. Milgram S. 1983. Obedience to authority: an experimental view. Harper Collins

Chapter 6.
1. Marmot M. 1994. Work and other factors influencing coronary health and sickness absence. Work and Stress, 8: 191 – 201.
2. Glasser, W. 1998. Choice Theory. Harper Perennial.
3. Collins J. 2001. Good to great: Why some companies make the leap and others don't. Harper Business.
4. Frankel V. 1946. Man's search for meaning. Washington Square Press.

Chapter 7.
1. Gray J. 1999. Venus and Mars starting over. A practical guide for finding love again after a painful break up, divorce or loss of a loved one. Harper Mass Market Paperbacks.

Chapter 8.
1. Maltz M. 1960. Psycho-cybernetics. Prentice Hall.
2. Bandler R and Grinder J.1975. The structure of magic. Science in Behaviour Books.

Chapter 9.
1. Gray J. 1999. Venus and Mars starting over. A practical guide for finding love again after a painful break up, divorce or loss of a loved one. Harper Mass Market Paperbacks.
2. Bandler R and Grinder J.1975. The structure of magic. Science in Behaviour Books.
3. Robbins A. Unlimited power. 1986. Simon and Schuster Ltd. Reprinted 2001.

Chapter 10.
1. Norris RW, Carroll D, Cochrane R. 1990. The effects of aerobic and anaerobic training on fitness, blood pressure and psychological well-being. Journal of Psychosomatic Research 34: 367-375
2. Handy C. 1998. The hungry spirit. RH Business.

Notes.

Notes.

Notes.

Notes.

Notes.

Notes.

Printed in the United Kingdom
by Lightning Source UK Ltd.
126139UK00002B/205/A